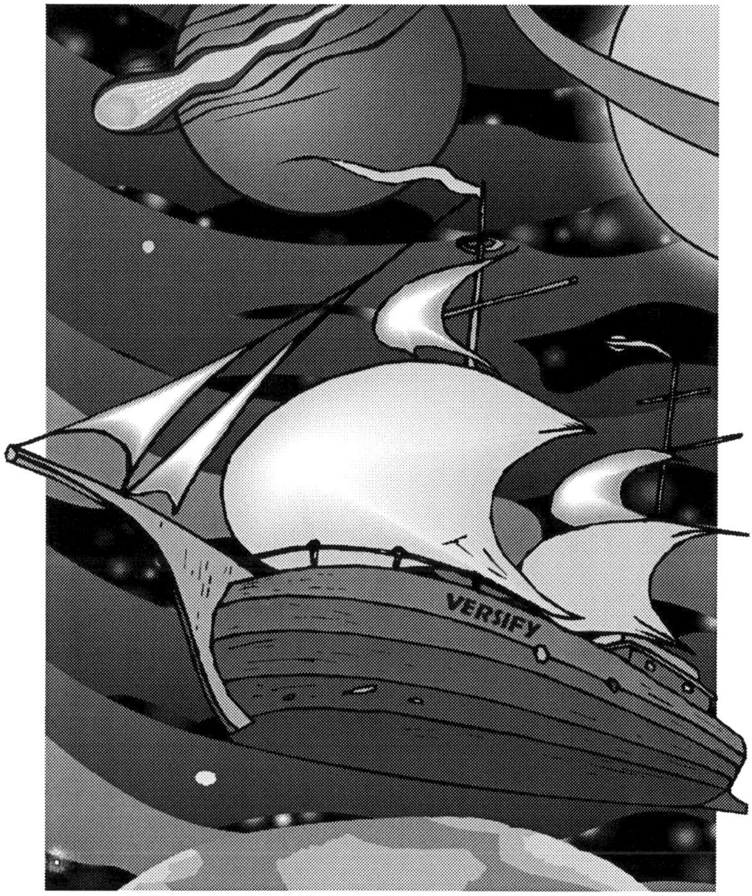

POETIC VOYAGES SOUTHERN ESSEX

Edited by Simon Harwin

First published in Great Britain in 2002 by
YOUNG WRITERS
Remus House,
Coltsfoot Drive,
Peterborough, PE2 9JX
Telephone (01733) 890066

HB ISBN 0 75433 492 9
SB ISBN 0 75433 493 7

FOREWORD

Young Writers was established in 1991 with the aim to promote creative writing in children, to make reading and writing poetry fun.

This year once again, proved to be a tremendous success with over 88,000 entries received nationwide.

The Poetic Voyages competition has shown us the high standard of work and effort that children are capable of today. It is a reflection of the teaching skills in schools, the enthusiasm and creativity they have injected into their pupils shines clearly within this anthology.

The task of selecting poems was therefore a difficult one but nevertheless, an enjoyable experience. We hope you are as pleased with the final selection in *Poetic Voyages Southern Essex* as we are.

CONTENTS

The Poems

Fireworks

Fireworks are banging in the sky
They are like a rainbow sparkling
Bonfires burning as hard as they can
Sparklers sparkling in the night
Catherine wheels swirling and turning
Rockets shooting in the sky
Frenzy fireworks scaring you
Canons firing
Shining silver
A meadow full of fireworks
Fireworks green and gold
Bang, pop, crash
And we always remember the fifth of November.

Emma Hawkes (7)
Brightside Primary School

Flower Seller

As the cold, wet winter nights pass,
I curl up in my corner, sleepless.
I close my eyes and dream
Of being rich, with somebody to love me.
The howl of the wind keeps me awake,
The rats nibble at my thin, ragged dress.
I wake up and buy flowers,
Then pick the rest.
I slowly walk to the city centre to sell them.
As people walk past,
I starve . . . I wish they would buy them,
So that I could eat tonight.

Laura Kettlewell (9)
Brightside Primary School

LIVING LIFE ON THE EDGE

With dark, dismal days
Living life on the edge
Each day I climb
The tunnel of death
Living life on the edge.

My broom is one hand
Death circles my brain
Each day I climb
The tunnel of death
Living life on the edge.

No friends, family or bed have I
And probably soon no pulse
As I climb the tunnel of death
Living life on the edge.

Each day and night
I wonder
If I will ever see
The brightness of the sun
Living life on the edge.

Emma Webb (9)
Brightside Primary School

DOLPHINS

Dolphins are so peaceful,
When they jump up high,
With their babies behind them,
Who love to jump up in the sky.

Baby dolphins are so cute,
And they are brilliant swimmers,
They talk to their mums with a very loud 'Squeak!'
And they can do tricks with their flippers.

Dolphins are so lucky,
When they are able to survive,
I love dolphins,
They have very peaceful lives.

Dolphins are my beauties,
They have love as well,
We have to care for animals,
In this world.

Roma Carmella Allport (7)
Brightside Primary School

THE CHIMNEY SWEEP BOY

Every day I climb the dusty, dingy chimneys,
My ears always ring.

Climbing, climbing through the soot,
I always blister and cut my feet.

Is it worth living?
No bed, no home, don't even have a shilling.

Misty, foggy, dark, dismal, cold -
Someone please help!

The streets are all I have;
I am terrified of everything.

In the blackness of the chimney,
Nobody ever sees me.

The wind blows,
Oh, if I was rich!

I wonder if I would see the terror
That I suffer now.

Ashley Dawe (10)
Brightside Primary School

Coal Miner's Hell

As I go down into the coal mine
I feel my bones shivering
As I go down into the wet coal mine
I hear deafening noises from people shouting at me.
Hell is down there.
As I go down I feel like I'm buried alive.

I have no home to keep me warm
Or no bed to have a good rest.
As I go down it grows darker.
It's cold down there.
I am really exhausted.
There is no one to care for me.

I'm so petrified that the heavy coal cart
Might crush my bones to death.
I feel like I'll never leave this place.
I'm not sure if I should be living.
I've got no food in me at all.
I'm starving to death.
It's a coal miner's hell.

Thomas Newman (9)
Brightside Primary School

Me

I have the same blue eyes as my nanny
I have the same nose as my mum's
I have my dad's fingers and thumbs
I also have the same feet as my grandad

I may have had a spot on my chin
And sometimes not get out of bed
But this is what my mum always has said
'Please and thank you and sorry,' yep, that's right
'Please and thank you and sorry.'

I may have lots of friends
I might be small, I might be mad
But what makes me particularly glad
Is just to be me.

Anna Parkins (8)
Brightside Primary School

Dreams Of A Street Child

In my cobbled bed I sleep,
I close my eyes and dream.
I dream of having a family
To cherish and care for me.
I dream of eating food, real and proper food.
But, alas, from that sweet dream
I fall into darkness.
Hanging down is a strip of love and care
As I grab that strip I wake.
I wake to find the streets plagued with rats
Nibbling my toes.
I wake to hear the sound of horses' hoofs
Clattering along, shattering my hopes
With a noise loud enough to wake the dead.
When, oh when will I die?
I fall back again
And dream.
I dream I am rich, sitting lovingly on Mama's knee
Or that I am the queen and I can do what I want.
From that dream I fall;
I land in the workhouse
Among the dingy corridors I roam
Walking forever on and on
Into the arms of God I dream.

Olivia Scott (10)
Brightside Primary School

FLOWER GIRL

I get up at six in the morning
And go to bed at eight at night
It's cold and damp where I sleep
In the street by the flower market
I'm very frightened
It is so noisy because the horse and carriage passes by
I have to have the flowers ready by seven
I sell them for one or two shillings
From the flower market.

I don't have a proper bed
I have a box to sleep in
I have only one very small blanket
I have gruel for lunch
Gruel for dinner
And gruel for tea
I have only the clothes I stand up in
I stop selling at eight
And go straight to sleep early
Or I will be late in the morning
And the flowers will be gone.

Kerry George (10)
Brightside Primary School

SIZES POEM

I may be small,
Which I think I am,
I may be tall,
As anyone can.

I may be fat,
But I don't think I am,
I may be as thin
As anybody can.

I may be small,
I may be tall,
But it doesn't matter for you and me,
Cos God made us all.

Fat, thin or in the middle,
It is inside which counts,
Not how fat or thin you are,
But love in large amounts.

Verity Butt (8)
Brightside Primary School

CLIMBING TOWARDS YOUR DEATH

Climbing up
Everlasting
Non-stop darkness
Falling soot
Climbing the shaft
Arms spread out wide
t's like a tunnel
An infinite tunnel
A tunnel of doom and sorrow
A tunnel of darkness
Surrounding me
A tunnel of living hell
In the shaft it sometimes feels
Like climbing towards your death.
Cold, musty
Fumbling in the dark
Preparing never to see sunlight again
Complete silence
Ever darkening
Like climbing towards your death.

Tom Barnes (10)
Brightside Primary School

A Coal Miner

In the blackness down the mine,
Anyone can come here, there's no time.
Dirty, cold, wet and damp
It would be better with a lamp.
The coal, making me squashed and scared
Thinking of rich people, cosy and cared.
Having no bed,
No cuddling ted,
No tone,
Or food,
No colour,
Or song.
In the darkness
I belong.

James Chauvin (10)
Brightside Primary School

The Road Sweeper Boy

I dream that I am rich
So I don't have to sweep roads
In freezing, cold weather
With only a thin ragged top
And tattered trousers

My job is very messy indeed
I just wish Lady Luck
Would replace the dirt
Of the street monster from Hell
With the comfort of a warm, clean home

I dream that I am rich
So that I don't have to sweep roads
In freezing, cold weather
I only wish for a bed
And warm clothes to wear.

Kyle Mayhew (9)
Brightside Primary School

Poor Child

I am living on the street,
I feel as though I'm going to weep.
No job I have, nothing to eat,
So I go scavenging on the street.
I pick pockets all day long
And then I hear the dinner gong.
But, alas, no food for me,
No tasty steak that I can see.
Not even gruel do I get.
The bakers won't even let
A single morsel touch my mouth,
But now winds blow from the south
As I lay in my cold, stone bed
Even without being fed
I really, really want a bun
Before the workhouse people come.
I really want to go to school,
I really want to have some gruel,
Or maybe a great big steak.
But now I awake
From a dream
And face reality.

Tom White (9)
Brightside Primary School

THE MILLS

Heads crushed
And fingers trapped.
Why am I here
In this dangerous place?
The mills.

I have only a small bed
To sleep in
And work
Twelve hours a day
In the mills.

Nobody to care
For me,
Nobody to love me
In the mills.

I wish I had a house
Of my own
But we don't
In the mills.

Kirsty Hough (9)
Brightside Primary School

THE TUNNEL

Every day and every night
I sit here all alone
In the dark, damp, gloomy tunnel
Waiting for the creatures of death of arrive
Clitter, clatter
Goes the deafening noise of the trailers.

There's no time for sleeping
Always listening out for the
Creatures of death to arrive
It's as though sunlight has been forbidden
Morning is always night.

Casey Evins (10)
Brightside Primary School

The Doors Of Hell

Dingy, misty and damp,
As I sit next to the doors of Hell,
I hear the deafening sound of a pickaxe,
The sound I know very well.

It's like being buried alive down here,
While I open the doors for the monsters to trundle in,
Sweat dribbles down my chest,
Sweat dribbles down my chin.

Sweat streams down my blackened face,
Leaving white, sorrowful trails behind it.

Will I ever see the light of day?
What is there to live for?
Will I ever get out of this black hole?
Will I ever see the end of . . .
The doors of Hell?

Sarah Morley (9)
Brightside Primary School

The Flower Girl

As I stand out in the wet, cold street
I hear deafening noises
All through the day
No home, no bed
I sleep on the hard, damp pavement
It chills me to the bone
In total darkness, all sorts of things
Come to nibble my toes
Early in the morning, as the horses trot past
I think of the rich people and their posh clothes
Will they ever notice me
Or will they pass me by
Forever?

Rebecca West (9)
Brightside Primary School

If I Was A Monkey

I would climb up a tree
Reaching for bananas
To eat for my tea

If I was a monkey
Leaping through the air
Playing with my friends
I don't even care.

Daniel Read (7)
Brightside Primary School

Barnado's Poem

As I walked
Through the streets
I saw sights I didn't want to see.
I saw a boy all in rags
Who stared at me with sad eyes
Cold, asleep in a wooden box
As I walked further through the streets
Many more caught my eye
Cold on that brittle road
With raging rats
And weeping child
I walked
Through the streets
Of shame.

Jonathon Allwood (10)
Brightside Primary School

Bonfire Night

Bonfires burn bright as can be,
Flames dance up and cackle with glee,
Sparklers fizz while rockets explode,
People gaze up from below,
Crash, bang is all you hear that night!
And you see the yellowish glow of the bonfire's light,
Then there is silence, no fireworks to be seen,
But the fireworks are still in everyone's dreams.

Hannah Neill (7)
Brightside Primary School

FLOWER GIRL

As the dark cramps me in the cold, cruel night
Always and forever
I smell the sweet scent of my flowers
That are sitting in their brown box.

People stop and see me sleeping
In the draughty, damp place
Near the corner of the workhouse.

Do they feel my wish?

I sit and I wish that I could
Rent a room in the inn
That is warm and light.

Emma Pryke (10)
Brightside Primary School

AUTUMN

Autumn days in the breezing weather
Chestnut shells shining up the trees
I cannot wait for the birds to be migrating
Poor, poor half-bare trees
Conkers are nice and shining brown
All the animals will be hibernating
Crystal conkers and acorns in their shells
I think I want to feed the little squirrels
Leaves go crispy, crunchy as I tread on them
Wet, wet leaves tickle my knees.

Pearlianne Corless (8)
Brightside Primary School

The Road Sweeper Girl

I dreamt that I was poor
And that I had no money at all
I could not be anything I wanted to be
I dreamt I was in a cold, dark room
And I had no bed
It was freezing cold
Playful rats nibbled at my toes
I could not get any sleep at all
I was working as a road sweeper girl
With only one shilling for my pay
So that is why I say
I was poor.

Chantelle Young (9)
Brightside Primary School

Autumn

Autumn, there is crystal grass
And rough, wet, crispy leaves
There is see-through fog and autumn air
Leaves are yellow, leaves are brown
There are golden sheaves of corn around
Birds migrating to another country flying
Swooping very softly
There are half-bare trees which have lost their leaves
Autumn time is here.

Anna Skaret-Ball (8)
Brightside Primary School

Alone

It's cold, black, dirty and wet
I have no quilt, only a sheet.
I sit by a hole
And feed the mouse cheese
That I found in the street.
Sadly I sit by the door,
Waiting for a knock
Waiting for people to help me.
I get frightened and scared,
With hardly any money,
No food, dirty water, nothing.
Even though I try
To get money by selling flowers.

Stephanie Woolmer (10)
Brightside Primary School

Chimney Sweep

I work by cleaning people's chimneys
My age is seven
I do not like doing this
I get scared doing people's chimneys
I get so cold, I freeze
I've fallen five times
I've broken my left arm before
And I've broken my left foot
I do not like doing this.

Grant Norrington (10)
Brightside Primary School

Flower Girl

I get up at 6.00
I'm ready at 6.30
I sell at 7.00
I sell the flowers
For 1 or 2 pennies
I live in one room
I have a mattress
And a cold blanket
I have gruel for breakfast
I don't have gruel for lunch
For I don't have lunch
But I do have gruel for dinner
I stop selling at 6.30
And go to bed at 7.30.

Tegen Ball (10)
Brightside Primary School

My Cat

I have a pet cat,
Her name is Turbo, fancy that!
Big and fluffy with dark brown fur
When I stroke her she starts to purr
She always sleeps upon my bed
But only after she has been fed
And when I'm happy she is glad
I love my cat, I love her so
She's my best friend, *Turbo!*

Kirsty Chapman (7)
Brightside Primary School

The Mine Worker

It's so cold down here in the mine,
I feel like I'm going to freeze.
I wait and wait until
I hear the coal truck coming
And then I open the door.
It's like endless hell down here.
It's dark, dingy, dismal and damp.
I get scared sometimes.
When I open the door
I think that a monster from hell
Is going to eat me.
I've got no home, no family,
No bed to sleep in.
I just stay down here in the mine,
Every day and every night.
I just wish I hadn't been born.

Daniel Bird (9)
Brightside Primary School

The Life Of A Chimney Sweep

Climbing chimneys is a fright
Especially when you climb at night
Sometimes I lie in the roads and sleep
I often hear poor orphans weep.

I am used to the smell of smoke
I sometimes breathe some in and choke
I always wish I had a mum
But I've got nothing . . .
And no one.

Matthew Holland (10)
Brightside Primary School

Autumn

Autumn days are crisp and cold,
Autumn leaves are frosty and frozen.
Lots of lovely sheaves of golden grain,
Because it's harvest time again.
Sparkly, shimmery, shiny grass,
Misty fog on the window glass.
Squirrels collecting acorns for their nest,
In winter it's their time to rest.
There is lots of harvest food like golden grain
And in autumn it's harvest time again.

Emily Wilkes (7)
Brightside Primary School

The Streets Of Shame

I walked the streets of shame today
And saw the sad faces of children
But other people were walking by
I asked them where they lived
And if they had food to eat
But they had to sleep out there
On the cold street
Of shame.

Georgia Clark (10)
Brightside Primary School

The Chimney Sweep

It is cold
I am scared
I've got
No bed
And no home
I have no money
I'm scared and
I tremble
I pray that
I don't fall
And only my elbow gets cut
As I climb higher
Higher, higher
I pray that I
Will see
Another day.

Craig Cosens (10)
Brightside Primary School

Monkeys

Monkeys look happy when they are playing
Swinging and swaying
They eat lots of bananas
They act like nanas
Monkeys live in the jungle
Because they are too big to live in a house
If they sit on a chair they will break it
They get heavier and heavier
They climb up trees a lot.

Callie Randall (8)
Burnham-On-Crouch Primary School

TEACHER

Teacher, teacher!
Sam fell over
And bashed
His head.

Teacher, teacher!
Adam has
Been sick
In his bed.

Teacher, teacher!
Jake made a cake
And he put it
On a rake.

Teacher, teacher!
Jamie is talking.

Be quiet!

Reese Sharpe (9)
Burnham-On-Crouch Primary School

POWER CUT

Under my bed I see a gloom,
Right there in such a messy room.
I find a car, it's black and white,
There in the distance, it's such a fright.
One more push, I see a glimmer,
There's my torch that shines and shimmers.
I crawl back out,
Then finally shout.
I see my cat,
It's caught a great, big rat.

Iain Sophie (11)
Burnham-On-Crouch Primary School

My Annoying Sister

How annoying is my sister?
If she went away I wouldn't miss her.

She is always shouting at me
But she never shouts at the other three!

She wears her hair in a bun
And I would say she hates fun!

She doesn't like what I watch on telly
And she tells me that my socks are smelly!

What big shoes, clump, clump, clump
And she is always in a grump.

Pizza is her favourite food
Sometimes she can be very rude!

She is quite good at art
And she can be very smart.

And she exercises a lot
And she made a horrible pot.

She likes her clothes plain
They're mostly the same.

She speaks to her boyfriend on the phone
And she has an Emma-free *zone!*

Emma Blake (9)
Burnham-On-Crouch Primary School

Teeth

My teeth are yellow
My teeth are white
My teeth are bad
But my teeth are bright

'Now open your mouth'
The dentist would say
And I would think in my head
No way!

Jamie Bache (9)
Burnham-On-Crouch Primary School

Stop Licking Your Lips

If you like chicken
Then you'll stop licking

Very chapped lips
Make it sore to eat chips

If you want the chicks
Then stop licking your lips

If you don't want them to rip
Then don't get a chapped lip

You've got to stop your tongue
When you're very young

If you want a kiss
Then give licking a miss

If your lips get sore and sticky
Put Vaseline on your lippy

So if your tongue should start to wander
Ask yourself and ponder
Is it really worth the risk
Just to lick your lips?

So before you lick
Think of a chip!

Kane Courtier (11)
Burnham-On-Crouch Primary School

Him

When he is walking
I see him talking
He picks his nose
And he likes to pose
He spits when he speaks
And his shoes they do squeak
For tuck he has cake
That his mum likes to bake
He thinks he is so clever
But his hand goes up, never!
His clothes they are posh
But does he ever get to wash?
He sings like a pig
And wears a wig
He reads a book
About Captain Hook
He has no friends
Because he wears a lens
He thinks he is posh
Because he has dosh.

Kasey Coppin (10)
Burnham-On-Crouch Primary School

My Best Friend

I've got a friend
Who is scared of the dark
He comes from Scotland
His name is Mark

It's fabulous and funny
To have a real, great mate
If I was a girl
I wouldn't ask him for a date

We are always playing games
Especially after school
When it comes to homework
We always use a tool

When it's snowy and cold
We go around skidding on the ice
And sometimes we fall over
Then we have to walk like mice.

Charlie Renwick (10)
Burnham-On-Crouch Primary School

I Know Someone

I know someone who is sometimes sad
I know someone who is sometimes bad
I know someone who is sometimes glad
I know someone who is sometimes mad
I know someone who has a dad
I know someone who has a dog
I know someone who trod on a frog
I know someone who has ten cats
I know someone who is afraid of rats
I know someone who looks like a monkey
I know someone who is very funky
I know someone who flies like a bird
I know someone who runs with the herd
I know someone who has a bunny
I know someone who likes honey
I know someone who screams like a ghost
I know someone who is a big host
I know someone who knows the times table
I know someone who lives in the stable
I know who they are, but do you?

Nicole Charlton (10)
Burnham-On-Crouch Primary School

Bridge Over Troubled Waters

The trees are bare but not for long
Because now it's spring
I look down on the river and he looks back at me
His shining eyes, his weedy hair of green and blue
His body of no shape
He never eats, he never drinks
He never sleeps or rests
After short amounts of time summer has began
With great bright suns of purple and yellow
As the sun goes over me and the river under
A group of ducks go meandering
As dragonflies are hovering
A rat, a toad, they all live here
Autumn comes, the leaves go brown
They start to fall jumping, leaping, dancing
Bubbling, frothing water, whirls beautiful colours
The swallows leave
The river is cold, now the tree coat is gone
Winter has arrived, the snow has come, he is icing up
His life is short, he will soon die but live again next spring.

Matthew Lis (11)
Burnham-On-Crouch Primary School

The Countryside

I see the hill far off on the horizon
A car travels down the woodland road
'Neath the creek I hear a croak of a toad
Cows in a field, grazing like bison.

The sun glows in the morning sky
Wind flows gracefully through the air
No more perfect moment to stare
At the countryside as the world passes by.

Tree upon tree stand before me
Mist in the next field and beyond
The creek's waterfall forming a pond
As woodland stretches as far as the eye can see.

Carl Beecroft (9)
Burnham-On-Crouch Primary School

THE PLAYGROUND

In the playground
Children play
In the playground
Colourful images
Hit the playground
As children fall and trip
Children run
Having fun
In the playground
Children skipping
Then when we're in
Children do PE
Come back out
At lunch time
Dinner bell rings
Time for lunch
Finish lunch
Come back out
Play a game
Whistle blows
Now the playground
Is dead!

Joshua Coleman (8)
Burnham-On-Crouch Primary School

FUN

My mum was funny
When my mum saw a bunny
I am having some fun in the sun
I had a cream bun
My friend was not having a good day
He didn't go on his date today
My friend had an excellent time
My friend found a dime
My brother went on his brilliant date
My brother cleaned his plate
I went on a ride, it was great
My friend went out with his mate
I went fishing
I did lots of wishing
I made a wish
I caught a fish
I made my mum happy
I was snappy
I had lots of fun when I was a baby
I could get ten pounds, maybe.

Michael Butcher (11)
Burnham-On-Crouch Primary School

MY PONY

Small and grey
With a silver mane
Bounty is my pony
She goes so fast
It makes me laugh
I love my little pony.

Alexandra Wood (7)
Burnham-On-Crouch Primary School

My Brother

I wrestle with my brother, he is sixteen
He always wins but I'm only eight
I don't know why he always wins
Maybe it's because he's a little bigger than me
  But I don't care!

I play football with my brother, he is sixteen
He always scores but I'm only eight
I don't know why he scores
Maybe it's because he's a little older than me
  But I don't care!

I race with my brother, he is sixteen
He always wins but I'm only eight
I don't know why he always wins
Maybe it's because he's a little faster than me
  But I don't care!

But at least I don't ride into ditches!

Helen Waller (9)
Burnham-On-Crouch Primary School

My Big Black Cat

My big black cat is ever so fat
When he lies down he covers the doormat
When he goes hunting he comes back with a mouse
And drops it right outside our house
We call him Zippy but sometimes Piggy
He likes to play, he likes to sleep
But most of all he likes to eat!

Paul King (9)
Burnham-On-Crouch Primary School

Best Friend

I've known my best friend for over three years
We've never ever been in tears
Her best animal is a horse
So is mine, well of course
Her favourite food is macaroni cheese
Get it away from me if you please
I go to her house most of the time
Although she sometimes comes to mine
Down the road on our bikes we ride
Me and my friend ride side by side
Purple is her favourite colour
She doesn't like black, that's even duller
She thinks Britney Spears is great
Her bedroom is never in a state
That's my best friend
Sorry my poem has come to an end.

Hayley Bassett (10)
Burnham-On-Crouch Primary School

Mrs Burchell

This lady has sparkly teeth
People never give her grief
She has never committed a crime
Gets to school on time
She is never sad
She is always mad
Sometimes glad
She is the best teacher I have ever had.

Daniel Simpson (10)
Burnham-On-Crouch Primary School

SCHOOL

School is good, school is bad
Whatever I do they're always mad
When my teacher drinks her tea
She spills it on her knee
She screams so loud
That no one is proud
And that's what is bothering me
Playtime is great
When I play with my mate
When the bells goes
We can't be late
Lunchtime is fun
When I eat my bun
Then it's back out to play in the sun
In the afternoon we must read
We go to the library for the books we need
After that we must write about everything we did last night
We had to write about the news
And give our very own views
Now at last it's time to go home
So I can ring my friend on the phone.

Danny Wallace (11)
Burnham-On-Crouch Primary School

MY GIANT

My giant's big
My giant's cool
My giant's very, very tall
I am short
I am cool
But I am very, very small.

Iona Coppin (8)
Burnham-On-Crouch Primary School

MY BEST FRIEND, SABINE

Sabine is my best mate in the world, that's great!
She is as sweet as honey and is always making me laugh.
Sabine is so funny, she is tiny but wild,
But still a nice child.

She has a laughing face,
Sabine can run very fast so she wins every race.
Sabine is my loyal friend and promises you can make,
secrets she can be trusted with and never will them break.
Sabine is modern with everything she wears.
She never will desert those whom she most cares.

Her eyes are big and bluey-green,
I don't think she ever could be mean.
Sabine always will be my best friend,
I hope she is with me.

Imogen Groves (10)
Burnham-On-Crouch Primary School

MY CAT FRED

I have a little cat
I call him Fred
He likes to curl up on my bed
All he does is eat and sleep
He likes lots of fish and plenty of meat
My cat Fred is very nice
He doesn't drink milk
He doesn't catch mice
All he does is lay on the mat
Until I give him his KiteKat.

Lucy Raven (7)
Burnham-On-Crouch Primary School

Mars

It seems a million miles away
Through cold and heat
But I know it's up there somewhere
And its name is like a sweet

It seems to be quite beautiful
With canals long and straight it's said
It has lots and lots of craters
And oh yes, the colour red

I would like to build a spaceship
And fly up to the stars
And maybe if I can find it
I would land on *Mars!*

Laura Dye (9)
Burnham-On-Crouch Primary School

On The M25

I hate the M25, it's boring
I hate the M25, it's always busy
I hate the M25, please help!

Ross Rawinsky (9)
Burnham-On-Crouch Primary School

Pounce

Pounce is my best friend
It's like he's alive

But he's not alive
He's the best.

Liam Argent (8)
Burnham-On-Crouch Primary School

THE SUN

The sun rises in the sky
Up and up and up so high
Millions of miles from the Earth
Up and up and up so high
In the middle of the day
The sun is so far away
But it won't stay.

In the afternoon the sun
Starts to go down
Down and down and down so low
It's near the evening waiting, waiting
Softly creeping, slowly, slowly
Into the evening.

It's the evening, evening, evening
The day has turned into dusk
The day has ended.

Jack Saunders (7)
Burnham-On-Crouch Primary School

MY BROTHER

My brother's girlfriend is called Alex
She's tall, he's small
She's good, he's bad
She's cute, he's ugly
I think they suit each other
Don't you?

Hayley Darkins (9)
Burnham-On-Crouch Primary School

Christmas Eve

Brush my teeth, go into bed
Have a kiss from my mum
Then I tuck myself in
Hear a little sound
It sounds like bells
It looks like a sleigh in the sky
With reindeers and presents
He comes down the chimney
'Ho, ho, ho!' he said
He had a big, white beard
I come down the stairs
He is gone
'Where is he?' I say
I went back to bed.

Laura Pursey (8)
Burnham-On-Crouch Primary School

Vast Countryside

Walking in the vast countryside
Relaxes me from head to toe
Fields are green, lakes are blue
Happiness goes through and through.

I walk along so happy all day
Then I see a car go the opposite way
A breath of smoke goes through my lungs
Then the taste slides on my tongue.

This world has turned full of disease
It's really upsetting with no fresh breeze
This land now rotten to the core
Will it ever be as pure as before?

Kate Pender (11)
Burnham-On-Crouch Primary School

Mars

M ar is
A
R otating planet in the
S olar system

M ars eats
A eros every
R otating day in the
S olar system

M ighty
A nd
R uthless but
Silly.

Joshua Beard (10)
Burnham-On-Crouch Primary School

Space

Floating
In
Space
Like an aeroplane
Seeing every planet in space
Just the best place in space
I
Just
Love
It!

Oliver Smith (8)
Burnham-On-Crouch Primary School

Imagination

In my corner
In my chair
I can be anyone
I can go anywhere

I'm Cleopatra
Queen of the Nile
Now I'm an athlete
I'll run for a mile

I'm Queen Victoria, 'We are not amused'
I'm Queen Elizabeth looking slightly bemused
I'm Catherine of Aragon, in a big crimson dress
Sitting in a palace, making a mess

And while I'm there . . .
No, I'm safe in my corner, in my chair.

Misha Rosenthall (10)
Burnham-On-Crouch Primary School

Falling Out With Your Friend

Best friends,
Falling out,
Walking away,
Not talking,
Falling out,
Not talking,
Go home,
Come to school,
Friends again!

Leanne Glover (9)
Burnham-On-Crouch Primary School

WINTER

The small breezes
The water freezes
I am glad
But it seems so sad

The bare trees
Now can see
How horrible life
Can really be

The snowflakes
Start to fall
As I throw my last ball
I go in and start to bake
Some more and more
Christmas cakes.

Elizabeth Vannuffel (11)
Burnham-On-Crouch Primary School

EARTH

E normous but not biggest
A nything to do
R ound
T all and wide
H ere on the Earth we all live

E verything is good
A round we travel
R avenous some people are
T iny and tall people are
H olds things you dream of.

Mark Westwood (9)
Burnham-On-Crouch Primary School

THE FERRY BOAT POEM

Bigger than buses, bigger than coaches,
Bigger and bigger as it approaches.
In the docks I see cranes lifting,
All the cargo they are shifting.

Every day you can see the ships,
Going in and out.
Cars and passengers getting on and off,
With lorries driving about.

I like the ships coming in and out,
I like to see them docking.
I like to see the sea rough,
So I can see the ferry rocking.

Lewis Whitmill (10)
Burnham-On-Crouch Primary School

I'M CALLING MY BEANIES

Snip, Chip, Prance and Leo
Stretch, Smokey, Oddball and Me.
I'm calling my Beanies
There are cats, dogs and all other creatures
Lots and lots of other Beanies
Why don't you get some?
There are fluffy ones, soft ones
Lots!
I'm calling my Beanies.

Olivia Rosenthall (7)
Burnham-On-Crouch Primary School

My Teacher's Name Is Mary

My teacher's name is Mary
And she is very scary
This could be cos she's hairy
Or is nothing like a fairy

She doesn't like big kids
Because they always fib
We always tried to hide
Because she knows we lied

My teacher likes to dance
And encourage us to prance
There is a slight hitch
Because the boys think she is a *witch!*

Elizabeth Knott (11)
Burnham-On-Crouch Primary School

School's Out

Our hour till school is out
I'll be glad there's no doubt
No more pencils, no more books
No more teachers' dirty looks
No more puffing with PE
No more boring ICT
History, geography, RE as well
It's boring learning how to spell
So everybody give a shout
Because boring school is out.

Katie Minett (11)
Burnham-On-Crouch Primary School

My Friend

My friend's got mouldy toes,
And a long nose.
Insects up above, that jump,
And she's kinda plump.
Shoes that don't fit,
At PE she has to sit.
My friend's got knotty hair,
She doesn't play fair.
She has manky teeth,
Loves to eat roast beef.
The poor dear,
Only one fear,
    Herself!

Kathryn Sangster (11)
Burnham-On-Crouch Primary School

Ghost

The chill ran up my spine,
There was no time,
But to scream and run,
No, not for fun.
I'd seen a ghost.

I was not fine,
I was only just out in time, phew!
It was not fun,
Just to run,
From that dreadful ghost.

Deanna Brash (10)
Burnham-On-Crouch Primary School

The Lost Song

There was a song I heard before,
It is there, then no more.
It whispered meanings in my ear,
And for me gave great cheer.
It could be lost at sea,
Far, far away from me.
Or right here in town,
If only I had written it down.
And there it was, right there,
In the window of St Clair.
We were rejoiced in love and harmony,
I sang my song very, very calmly.

Alice George (10)
Burnham-On-Crouch Primary School

S Club 7

S Club 7, S Club 7
I never had a dream come true
And then along came you
Along came you, a group of seven
And now we're all in S Club heaven
Jo, Tina, Hannah and Rachel
Jonathan, Bradley and Paul
You're the best
You beat the rest
S Club 7, S Club 7.

Daniella Smith (10)
Burnham-On-Crouch Primary School

The House Of Horror

I was in the a spooky house
There was a squeaky mouse
I opened a door
I couldn't believe what I saw
I saw some guts
Which looked like nuts

Around the dirty room
Could do with a broom
Cobwebs everywhere
Hanging around there
Broken pictures, broken chairs
It's enough stress to pull out your hair.

Rats there, mice here
Creepy crawlies everywhere
What a dirty, spooky house it is.

I'm glad I don't live there.

Craig Lawrence (10)
Burnham-On-Crouch Primary School

The Shining Moon

The shining moon gleams through the night
But when it's day it doesn't look bright
The moon shines on all the thieves
As they make their way along the leaves
The moon shines on the people as they sleep
Not a creature or person will peep
Only the sleepy, howling dog
Will see everything on the log.

Louise Mansfield (10)
Burnham-On-Crouch Primary School

Bethany

I love her blue eyes
and her long blonde hair
Her little round nose
and her skin so fair.

Her freckles are light
but can fade for a while
Her clothes are so bright
as bright as her smile.

Her necklace is gold
and her nature is sweet
I think she's the best girl
that you could ever meet!

Leanne Parsons (9)
Burnham-On-Crouch Primary School

Planets

Pluto, the furthest from the sun
A small blue dot in the sky
It's full of rock
Deeply frozen like a freezer
Its moon is locked together with gravity
Earth, a planet full of life forms
Birds, humans, horses, all in one big sphere
The sun, a massive humming ball of fire
Blazing, sizzling ball of hot, boiling gas
But it all starts off with one big *bang!*

Mark Poynter (9)
Burnham-On-Crouch Primary School

War

Silent and still I float through the salty mist
I play with my dolphin friends as we swim and twist
We speed past a swordfish who looks very profound
Splashing through the water we hear a muffled sound.

I swam to the surface to find a dreadful sight
Army troops everywhere shouting 'Fight, fight, fight!'
I had once seen a child playing ball
But now I see not a happy human at all.

People in the sea floating everywhere
I swan right into one which gave me a scare
I thought of my friends playing down in the sea
Then I thought why can't humans be like dolphins and me?

I'm swimming back to my dolphin friends
And I'm telling them never to go up there again
They're asking me why they are not allowed to go up there
Just then a man begins to sink, that is why you must take care.

Grace Francis (11)
Burnham-On-Crouch Primary School

Fish

Watching fish swim around
Nibbling stones on the ground
Fish can do somersaults in the waters blue
They can go swimming every day
Not like you!
Time for tea, there's fish today
'No thanks Mum, I feel sick!'

Naomi Brash (8)
Burnham-On-Crouch Primary School

CRAZY

I'm crazy, I'm loopy-loo, I have not got a clue
I've got a mum, she hears me play my organ
All day with you

Crazy though it may seem, this organ's got a crazy theme
The beat is loud, the tune is sweet
And I'm tapping my groovy feet
My shoes are cool and my clothes are small
I make a beat with my light feet.

My uncle Luke has a flute and it makes a toot
So now I know there's a crazy flute with my uncle Luke
So now I play my organ with the toot of my uncle Luke's crazy flute
Now I say to myself, I am not crazy like my uncle Luke.

Sam Hughes (11)
Burnham-On-Crouch Primary School

OUR FAT CAT

Sleeping peacefully
Noisy, cosy
Fat cat.

Chasing, racing
Calling, falling
Fighting, biting
Fat cat.

Struggling, cuddling
All sort
Eating, sport
Our fat cat.

Claire Dallimore (10)
Burnham-On-Crouch Primary School

TIME

Time no one understands,
We watch the clock's tiny hands.
We waste special hours,
We don't understand its powers.

As the seconds tick on by,
We will laugh, we will cry.
We don't realise that this is how,
Our lives are happening now.

So let's make the most of it,
And start to do our own bit.
And make some people's spirits high,
While the seconds go ticking by.

Megan Mullins (11)
Burnham-On-Crouch Primary School

THE BEACH

The beach is still and quiet now
Crowds flocked onto the sand in the day
The sea was cold and wet
But people still swam in the water
The beach sat there and watched them
As they splashed in the waves
Waiting for them to landscape the sand
With their hand spades and buckets
Waiting for the tide to wash it away
Waiting for the sun to go down
And the people to go home.

Isla Evans (9)
Burnham-On-Crouch Primary School

THE SUN

The sun is a yellow beach ball
That has been kicked high into the sky
The sun is a lump of sand
That's been thrown at a blue can
The sun is a bit of orange paint
That's been dropped on a blue tablecloth
The sun is a circle someone has drawn on some blue paper
The sun is a person getting up and going back to bed
The sun is an orange on a blue tablecloth
The sun is a bit of candle wax that's been dropped
On a blue tablecloth
The sun is a light bulb on a blue ceiling.

Kieron Pritchard (9)
Burnham-On-Crouch Primary School

FOOTBALL

The crowd roar
The players cheer
They're running up
They're here
A goal!
The crowd go crazy
But there is an open goal
Up the other end
But they missed
And they went crazy.

Stuart Worboys (8)
Burnham-On-Crouch Primary School

My Birthday

It's my birthday tomorrow
I'm really excited
I want it to be tomorrow
Party poppers
And even streamers
Mum is shouting
Bedtime
Yippee
This time tomorrow
I will be partying
I really can't wait.

Olivia Benson (8)
Burnham-On-Crouch Primary School

The Sun

The sun is the hottest of them all
It's round like a ball
A giant star
Like the eighth par of a golf course
A galloping horse
In the sky a cherry pie
Caring, round, hot and *big*
The boss of space
Keeping us in a case
A peeping eye.

Lewis Vaughan (9)
Burnham-On-Crouch Primary School

A Snowy Christmas

One morning I woke up
It was . . . *Christmas*
My mum was already excited
Saying wake up and look at the snow

I got up and went to the window
There was white, crispy snow for miles and miles
Believe me, I smiled.

Philippa Gibbs (7)
Burnham-On-Crouch Primary School

Fish

Fish swim beneath the sea
Fish swim and, like birds, are free
In the deep they hide a lot
To get away from us ugly lot.

Annabelle Hobbs (7)
Burnham-On-Crouch Primary School

The Car

The car is shiny,
The car is blue,
But my dad is dirty.

Helen Martin (8)
Burnham-On-Crouch Primary School

Smiley Faces Everywhere

Once in my street
I saw some faces
Some smiley faces
Once in my street
I saw some faces
Some wicked faces
One in my street
I saw some people play
Once in my street
I saw some people fighting.

Sarah Dallimore (7)
Burnham-On-Crouch Primary School

Rocks

Rocks are big and rocks are small
Rocks are sharp and blunt
Rocks are sparkling in the sun
Rocks are heavy and light
Rocks are smooth and rough.

Charlotte Smith (9)
Burnham-On-Crouch Primary School

Giants

Giants are as tall as a skyscraper
Giants are as slow as a tortoise
Giants are as heavy as a cliff
But this giant is my friend
I wish it would crush the school.

Emily Woloszczuk (9)
Burnham-On-Crouch Primary School

My Beanie

My cat Flip is mad to be a Beanie
Come on Flip, Tiger, Glow, The End and The Beginning
We can go down to the park
The moon is up and we can go home
The Beanies are best and good fun
Amy loves Beanies and we had a cookie
We can go to sleep and Beanies can do anything for you
Come on Flip, Tiger, Glow, The End and The Beginning
Let's go!

Amy Coppin (7)
Burnham-On-Crouch Primary School

My Hamster

My hamster's small
It plays with a ball
It never stops until it pops
My hamster's great because it's late
It's getting fed and getting to bed.

Thomas Doe (8)
Burnham-On-Crouch Primary School

My Cat

I've got a cat and its name is Bow
He's not very fast and he's not very slow
He's not very fat and he's not very thin
He jumps in tins and he jumps in bins.

Hannah Beard (8)
Burnham-On-Crouch Primary School

MOUNTAIN ISLAND

See all the rocks polished by the sea,
See the big, tall, thin, airy trees,
See all the mountains that are shining in the sun,
See all the people on the beach,
See the lovely sun shining bright,
See the blue . . . whole . . . sky,
See the green grass reflecting in the sun,
I wish there were lots of these beaches and mountains
    And most of all, the weather.

Nic Gandy (9)
Burnham-On-Crouch Primary School

THE WORLD

The world is round
The world is big
The world is green and blue
It has a sun and galaxies
That are spinning around it too.

Sophie Smith (9)
Burnham-On-Crouch Primary School

MY CAT

My cat is soft
My cat is cute
My cat is small
My cat is brown and black
I love my cat.

Holly Seager (8)
Burnham-On-Crouch Primary School

Motor Cross

I love motor cross
Hear the engine roar
Go, go, go
Then they're off

I love motor cross
And the smell of petrol
Mud goes everywhere

I love motor cross
18, ha that's my dad
He has won, yippee.

Geoffrey Parr (8)
Burnham-On-Crouch Primary School

My Budgie

My budgie talks
And plays just like me
But in the morning he's like an alarm
Because he chirps at 6 o'clock
My budgie won't be quiet, not one little bit.

Charlotte Sarti (8)
Burnham-On-Crouch Primary School

Super Bunny

I wake up
I let my rabbit out of its cage
It zooms across the garden
And hides behind the shed.

Ben Baker (8)
Burnham-On-Crouch Primary School

PE

We play outside
We have a lot of fun
We skip sometimes
But we all have fun
We play ball all the time
We play bench ball too
But we all have fun.

Rachel Warboys (8)
Burnham-On-Crouch Primary School

My Dog Jody

My dog Jody rolls all over the carpet
My dog Jody is really scatty
My dog Jody skids all over the floor
My dog Jody pounces up at me
When we come in from school
And knocks me flying.

Matthew Bovis
Burnham-On-Crouch Primary School

The Micro Scooter

My micro scooter
I let my friends play on it
It's like zoom, zoom
I fell off it once or twice
My micro scooter.

George Somers (8)
Burnham-On-Crouch Primary School

In The Dark

In the dark it's soundless, nobody is around
Just you and your toys crawling around
It is in the middle of sunset and sunrise
Through the curtain it glows at night
It's murky and dim
Cats can see in the dark
There might be somebody around looking
In the gloomy, murky night!

Jade Koenig (9)
Burnham-On-Crouch Primary School

City

In the city people going to work
People waking up in the city
People at work getting on with their work
People pushing and charging past
Children going to school on the school bus
When you're in the city remember one thing
Stay away from strangers.

Karl Swanborough (8)
Burnham-On-Crouch Primary School

Pluto

P luto is the smallest planet in the solar system
L ike a full stop in blue pen on black paper
U nder and over our planets and Pluto watches our Earth
T he ninth planet is Pluto
O ver the sky Pluto lies.

Tahn Bavin (10)
Burnham-On-Crouch Primary School

PLUTO

Pluto is far from the sun
And the smallest of the planets
Pluto is deep frozen
And a rocky place
Pluto's orbit is far from circular
And Pluto is a planet that was last found.

Ruba Shofique (10)
Burnham-On-Crouch Primary School

AT THE SEASIDE

At the seaside
I play with my ball
At the seaside
I have great fun
At the seaside.

Philippa Branchett (8)
Burnham-On-Crouch Primary School

EARTH

Earth is the third planet away from the sun
It spins round giving us day and night, it gives us life
It's a great big ball, green and blue
It holds me and you.

Alice Hasket Smith (9)
Burnham-On-Crouch Primary School

Pluto

Pluto is the furthest from the sun
The smallest planet that's been found
A nice light blue colour, duller than the sun
It was not found when the planets had begun
It's a frozen planet, rocky too
Looks like a ball floating in the sky.

Hayley Tammaro (10)
Burnham-On-Crouch Primary School

Venus

Venus, Venus filled with gas
Venus, Venus not that bad
Venus, Venus is not sad
Venus, Venus is so glad
Venus, Venus is so big
Venus, Venus is so, so slow.

Danny Howell (9)
Burnham-On-Crouch Primary School

Mars

Hot as burning fire
Red as the sun
Spins round the sun like a spinning top
Burning its flaming fire away
Showing off its lovely red coat.

Yazmin Way (9)
Burnham-On-Crouch Primary School

EARTH

Earth is where we all live
Creatures great and small
All together on this planet
Everyone and all
We are joyful, we have fun
On Earth with everyone
Earth is round like a ball
Look around with everything
And everyone.

Karly Moule (9)
Burnham-On-Crouch Primary School

LEAVES

Leaves falling
Red and brown
Off the tree
Jump on them
Crick, crack
Crick, crack.

Gemma Ball (9)
Burnham-On-Crouch Primary School

SUN

The sun is a hot star
And very, very far
It's a ball of gas
A plate of hot mash
People say it began with a *bang!*

Gemma McLoughlin (9)
Burnham-On-Crouch Primary School

My Teacher

Sometimes my teacher is cheerful,
Sometimes she's tearful,

She always looks smart
Even after art.

She's a whizz at sums
She doesn't even use her thumbs.

Addition, subtraction, multiplication, division
She always uses her vision.

She loves PE
And inspires ICT

She thinks she's funny
And she's a mummy

In geography and history
Which to me is a mystery

She tells us all about the past
And tries to make us work so fast

But best of all
She works at my school

And teaches us
Without a fuss.

Emily Hockings (10)
Burnham-On-Crouch Primary School

Pets

I've got a dog
His name is Bog
He likes to eat
He chases cats
All over the place
He's got a collar
As big as he can swallow
He's as big as . . .
Canary Wharf
His fur is as long
As the longest branch
But he's as cute
As cute, as cute
Well as cute as
Nothing really
There're not just one kind of dog
There's loads like my dog
Anyway, got to go, bye!

Amy Mount (10)
Coppice Primary School

Space Voyage

The boat was floating along in space
No one to wash its decks or scrub its stern again
The sails are torn, the stars are sharp
The mist covers the boat from head to toe
The solar wind blows and blows so the ship
just keeps going and going
The wood's rotating so the ship has ended its trip
As it floats around in space and looks down at us
Someone, somewhere is looking up as well.

Courtney Gwatkin
Coppice Primary School

MY DOG

I've got a dog
and his name is Bog.
He likes cats,
sitting on doormats.
The dog is fat like the cat.
We don't like the cat
because he ate our rat.

The dog got a collar
as big as a dollar.
He likes Pedigree Chum
because it's like his bum.

There's no dog
as loud as my dog.
He races the dog next door,
comes back and lays on the floor.
He hates the door bell,
when it rings when he's not well.
He's tall like a wall,
he's loud but
makes me proud.

Dominic Prasad
Coppice Primary School

THE ALIENS

There are little green aliens
Flying in the air
And a funny little sound
As they lift up off the ground.

With their crazy blue hair
And their little mushy food
They have silver and gold houses
They really are a bunch of cool dudes.

Their big, blue smiles
And their yellow and gold suckers
They are the real tops
And they grow their own crops.

They have funny yellow grass
They have a funny little class
I love these little Martians
'Cause I am one!

Moira Clarke-Moisley (10)
Coppice Primary School

Boats

All the boats go sailing by,
In the blazing blue sky.
I can see the big blue whales,
I can see other boats putting up their sails.
While I was on the ship,
I had a slip
And did one big flip,
I fell in the salt water,
While thinking of my daughter.
I tried to climb up the wood,
And kept my grip for as long as I could.
Then I lost my grip,
And went for another little trip.
While I was choking,
I realised I was floating.
While I was in the ocean,
They poured in some potion.

Jamie Chinery (11)
Coppice Primary School

I'D LOVE TO BE A POP STAR

I'd love to be a pop star
and buy a flashy car
I'd like to shout out high-pitched notes
and buy designer leather coats!

I'd love to be a pop star
to travel near and far
Singing on all the stages
and collecting a lot of wages!

I'd love to be a pop star
and drink in a trendy cocktail bar
I'd love to go to number 1
to show all the hard work I had done!

Zoë Hindle (11)
Coppice Primary School

DOGS

Dogs are cute,
Dogs are playful,
My dog plays a flute
And makes me cheerful!

Dogs are funny,
Dogs are *loud*
When it's sunny
He makes me proud.

Dogs are like doormats,
They don't like the door bell!

Sarah Badger (11)
Coppice Primary School

Boats

The boats are sailing round looking for the beach ahead
as they talk their speech.
They're shouting 'Captain, Captain, island ahead!'
The whales are swimming in the sea as they slaughter.
The boat is floating as its sailing through the ocean.
The sails flap as the gales get worse.
The waves are bad, as the sailor saves the captain's life.
The captain says 'You saved my life, thank you.'
The crew got seasick after terrible gales and winds
as they get off the boat.
Their holiday is over as the boat starts to sink
as all the people wink.

Jake Donovan (10)
Coppice Primary School

Spaceships

It is wicked to see them fly like birds in space,
Or be in the crew,
The feeling you get when you lift off,
You wonder if you are going to meet aliens.

If you do, you wonder if they will kill you or not,
If they invade your ship.
Rocks flying in space, dodging them like a computer game.
I would love to shoot other spaceships,
So you can see that a spaceship is a good place.

James Brown
Coppice Primary School

Space

Space - never-ending and going on and on
All we know of it is nine planets and the sun
Space - full of life and full of stars
Full of planets - Venus, Jupiter and Mars
Space - black, goes out further and further,
Some planets we know could be bigger than Jupiter
Space - comets, asteroids and shooting stars
Travelling, speeding and firing past
Space - Venus is hot, Pluto is cold but Earth is just right
Sun gives us heat and light
Space - who knows what lies unexplored
For us to discover beyond the stars
Space.

Mark Hatt (11)
Coppice Primary School

The Moon

The moon sits high in the sky,
just as if it could fly.
A ball of yellow,
looks lovely and mellow.
The moon shines,
while we drink and dine.
It puts on an air of grace,
as it hovers up in space.
The craters come together in a clan
to form what looks like a face of a man!

Caroline Dulson (10)
Coppice Primary School

LET'S DANCE

I dance to the beat of music,
I dance to the flow of slow music,
You can dance high, you can dance low,
I start getting faster with the beat,
I get a part in a play called 'The Last Part in Dance.'

I feel the flow of slow music getting slower as we speak,
I use the tip of my toes, I raise my leg high in the air,
It is dead straight.
It's fun being a dancer so you feel the dance flowing past,
I end in a pose, everyone claps and cheers,
They throw flowers while we bow.

Katie Jackson (11)
Coppice Primary School

SKY

I wake up in the morning and see the bright, hot sun
appearing through the white, clear clouds.
I can see the beautiful, tiny birds soaring
through the blue, bright sky.
I look out the window, the red hot sun shines
on my warm, pale face.
I can feel the hot sun beating on my cool face.
The sun disappears and it gets cooler and stars appear.
I look up and see the bright, white moon
sitting still in the dark, black sky.
I see the glimmery stars lighting up the lonely city.

Hannah Clark (10)
Coppice Primary School

HOLIDAY POEM

I went to the airport with my suitcase,
We took some money, it was very, very sunny.
We sunbathed on the sand and got a tan,
I love the sea, me!
I jumped and reached,
It was lovely and sunny on the beach!

Jamie-Lee Murphy
Coppice Primary School

FOOTBALL

Happiness for me is football!
I score all the goals, I am the best,
You watch me I'll beat the rest;
You'll see me play on TV,
Superstar that's me,
Scoring, earning until I'm rich.
At last I'll walk off the pitch.

Ryan Cariello (10)
Deneholm CP School

ANGER

When I get angry I storm off
but my friend only goes when pushed
I can be just as stroppy as those around me
I get mad with my brother when he moans for nothing
I get mad with my mother when she tells me to do my room
I get mad when my teacher tells me to stop talking
but I'm most angry when my mum tells me to clean up my room.

Bryony Brennan Welsh (10)
Deneholm CP School

Danger In The Sea

The jellyfish squirms beneath the sea,
I know it's there just waiting for me.
I can see it behind the slimy seaweed,
Help is what I want, it's what I need.

I can't swim against the water,
My feet can't touch the sand.
Oh what I'd give to reach and stand
On welcoming dry land.

What's that in the distance, is it a boat?
I hope it is, I must stay afloat.
Too late, the current is pulling me down,
The silence is pressing against my ears,
Drowning is one of my very worst fears.
'Help!' is the last word that I said,
I know it now, I know that I'm dead.

Katrina Hall (10)
Deneholm CP School

My Life

My life can be lonely,
My life can be sad,

My life can be happy,
Sometimes I'm glad.

Most of my life I have been asthmatic,
I'm also a nightmare because I'm hyperactive.

I really like to read books,
But I don't really care how I look.

Gavin Bishopp (11)
Deneholm CP School

What Pet Shall I Choose?

I went to the pet shop to buy a new pet
But kept wondering and thinking which one shall I get?

The first thing I saw was a rabbit, with snow-white fur
and blazing red eyes
And a fat, old guinea pig eating a mouldy piece of cucumber
covered in flies.

I brought them both home but what did they do?
They escaped from the cage and nibbled on Dad's shoe!

So I took them both back in a little old cage,
Then looked at a cute cat and a dog barked with rage.

So I brought them both home but guess what they did?
The cat ripped the sofa while the dog scared next-door's kid!

So I bought some fish instead but fish were boring just like Mum said.

Back to the pet shop for the last time and that's it
I couldn't decide so I got in a fit.

The last in the pet shop, I hadn't looked at
Was an everlasting eating hamster all smelly and fat.

That smelly, fat hamster does not look like fun,
'Mum, I think I've decided I'll go without one!'

Deanna Dove (9)
Deneholm CP School

My Pet Rabbit

My rabbit's name is Trixy
He always licks me
He's brown
He doesn't always act like a clown
He hops around all day long

I love Trixy so much
My sister loves him too much
He sleeps in his cage all alone
I always moan
He can't talk on the phone.

Michelle Cross (11)
Deneholm CP School

Gran

Gran's unconscious,
Nearly dead,
Lying still on the hospital bed.

Gran's on a life support machine,
Who knows what will happen to her.

It's been two days now and no reply,
It's obvious to me she's going to die.

I sit and wait anxiously,
Waiting to know if she's OK.

When out of the blue a loud sound begins,
It's coming from that machine,
It's a loud beeping noise,
What does it mean?

Then the nurse comes rushing in
And tells me to go out.
I wait ten minutes or more,
Then the nurse says 'I'm sorry
I have bad news . . . she's gone.'
'What do you mean, she's gone?' I cried.
'Gran's dead,' Mum replied.

Andrea Chalmers (11)
Deneholm CP School

AVALANCHE!

Steadily, slowly climbing up
No more drinking from a nice, hot cup
Oh no! A shout has set it off
Now is not the time to cough
Rumbling! Tumbling! Down the peak
I can't stop now, I can't be weak
I really wish I didn't lie
But it's too late, I'm going to die
Goodbye Mum and goodbye Dad
They will be so sad, they might go mad!

My eyesight's leaving me,
The darkness has thickened
There is no hope
And my heart has sickened.

Sophie Lakin (10)
Deneholm CP School

SCOT THE DOG

I'm a lonely dog
A sad dog but
I'm not a mad dog

I'm a cute dog
A slow dog
And I'm coming to my end

Now I'm a dead dog
A not fed dog
And here I lay on the floor.

Frazer Merrick (10)
Deneholm CP School

Happiness

Happiness for me,
Sitting down on Sunday and watching TV.
I love to watch wrestling you see,
That is the best part of the weekend for me.
Then another week, then Friday comes round.
Friday watching TV is where I will be found.
Watching Friends and Raw,
Lots of TV at the weekend and even more.

Jordan White (11)
Deneholm CP School

Spring

Spring is the time for new beginning
Animals are born, flowers blooming, birds tweeting
Everything has a new beginning
New life, new flowers
Leaves turn green
Easter's coming.

Jamie Rose Smith (11)
Deneholm CP School

Stress

Stress is like a ball of pain that pushes into your head
It thumps like a headache
Then it makes me cry
As if I have a nasty pain
So please don't make me angry or give me pain.

Samantha Garnham (11)
Deneholm CP School

Lonely Dog

I am an old dog, cold dog, sad dog alone
I am a hungry dog, unlucky dog
I only want a home.

My legs are old and weary
They've never had a walk
I wander and wander
For I long for someone to talk.

I dream of a sleep beside the fire
I dream and dream, for I always tire
Every day I slowly fade
Because I was not made to be alone.

Alone, alone, alone I will go
For I will always have an empty bowl.

I am an old dog, cold dog, sad dog alone
I am a hungry dog, unlucky dog
I only want a home!

Faye Butterfield & Katie Bilton (11)
Deneholm CP School

My Brother David

My brother David is smaller than me
He can't lift me very easily
He can't lift me up, he has tried and tried
He thinks I have got something heavy inside.

Nicole Turner (10)
Deneholm CP School

IMAGINATION

This is not my real life
This is just fantasy
This person is not real
This hand is not real
But is just like my imagination
I am surfing on the sea.

They have just zapped me into lava
I am sliding down a volcano
Now I'm gaining speed
Smash into the ground
And into the trees
Zap, I wake up
With no memory of what happened.

Ben Kelly (11)
Deneholm CP School

MY DAD

My dad lives faraway
I miss him every day

I love him so much
I miss him too much

It's true, it's true, I miss him
I hope he misses me
My dad I never see

I talk to him on the phone
He never ever moans

I love him
I hope he loves me!

Becky Magnurson (11)
Deneholm CP School

The Lost Boy

You go to school with teachers and helpers too,
how could they cope with a child like you?
You came from a home which didn't really care,
half the home was really bare.
You didn't go out and play in the street,
there wasn't a child you could ever meet.
You couldn't believe it when you saw the first sight
and you stayed awake half the night.
You couldn't stop thinking about the children you'd seen,
but some of the children seemed very mean.
Next you heard a bell start to ring,
then you heard somebody sing.
Next came a mighty boom
which told you to run to your classroom.

Rachel Glover (11)
Deneholm CP School

Red Is The Colour Of . . .

Red is the colour of hate
Red is the colour of anger
Red is the colour of danger
Red is the colour of fire
Red is the colour of blood
But also
Red is the colour of love
Red is the colour of hearts
Red is the colour of lips
Red is the colour of the sun
Red is the colour of cherries
So red has got two sides
A bit like Jekyll and Hyde.

Daniel Cowlbeck (11)
Deneholm CP School

ANGER

Anger is so bad
But some things really make me mad
I might get blamed if I am at home
When I've done nothing wrong
And then I go upstairs all alone
I feel anger deep inside
That's because my sister has lied
'Is this true?' is what my teacher said
When that was what she read
Katrina says that I'm a torment
But that's something that wasn't meant
But now Katrina is writing her side
Perhaps I was wrong
Maybe I lied.

Gareth Hall (10)
Deneholm CP School

RED

Red is anger
Red is hot
Red is fire
Red is blood
Red is the colour of my heart
Red is a rose
Red is bright
Red is red on a shepherd's delight
Red is a Ferrari winning a race
Red is a devil
But the best red of all is Manchester United.

Andrew Swash (11)
Deneholm CP School

PETS

Pets are playful
Friendly and loveable
Furry animals
Fluffy animals
All kinds for everyone

Dogs, hamsters, fishes and cats
All the way up to rats

The spotty ones
The stripy ones
The ones with only one colour
The ones with patches
The ones with scratches all over their body
The ones that match
The ones we catch
Doing their business in our back gardens

Pets are playful
Friendly and loveable
We all like to have *pets.*

Rebecca Portch (9)
Henry Green Primary School

DO AS YOU'RE TOLD!

Do as you're told!
Brush your hair
Sit on your chair
Do as you're told!

Behave!
Stop rummaging the place
Sometimes I wish I was in space
Behave!

Stop that!
Don't pick your nose
Don't bite your toes
Stop that!

Behave!
Don't play with your food!
She's not in the mood
She meant what she said
Now I've got to go to bed.

Tommy Roberts (9)
Henry Green Primary School

GHOST

Dark,
Dark,
It's really dark,
On my own it's scary,
Strange,
Strange,
It's really strange,
On my own it's scary,
Spooky,
Spooky,
It's really spooky,
On my own it's scary,
Shadow,
Shadow,
There's a shadow,
Quick,
Quick,
It's a ghost,
Aaarrghh!

Jade Bardwell (9)
Henry Green Primary School

ABC

AAAAA
BBBBBBB
CCCCCCCCC
At nine o'clock I go to school
To learn my ABC
I sit there at my desk so still
Wishing it was three
My teacher shouts please concentrate
Or you a dunce will be
But concentrate is hard to do
When what is on my mind
Is how to say but please Miss
I've left my lunch behind
XXXXXXXXX
YYYYYYY
ZZZZZ.

Jodie Emms (10)
Henry Green Primary School

I Spy

I spy
a pie
I saw it float in the air
and saw it turn into a pear
I spy
a pair of pies
I saw them float again
and down they came from the air
and fell onto my teacher's hair!

Charlotte Bardwell (8)
Henry Green Primary School

POEMS

Poems can be about sweets
Poems can be about noisy streets
Poems are a treat
Poems are really neat

People like poems, I know I do
Others don't, they're like monkeys in the zoo
Everyone's different, some like them, some don't
Most boring people won't!

Danielle Murphy (11)
Henry Green Primary School

ANIMAL POEM

Dogs bark on Noah's Ark
Birds tweet like the heartbeat of your heart
Snakes hiss like the power of your kiss
Hippopotamus snore like people knocking on your door
Flies cry like people eating pie.

Richard Lee (8)
Henry Green Primary School

MY FAMILY

My mum is groovy, cool,
My dad is Taurus the bull,
My sister is nice and tall,
My brother is silly and a fool,
My sister's son is crazy and silly.

Emma Louise (9)
Henry Green Primary School

WELCOME TO THE HAUNTED HOUSE!

Step in through the rusty gates
Be quiet as a mouse
We're going to sneak and take
A peek inside the haunted house!

Ghosts are hooting in the hallway
Ghostly ghouls lurk on the stairs
Imps and sprites have pillow fights
To catch you unawares!

In the kitchen there's a wizard
Making slug and spider pies
They're for a special meal -
A Hallowe'en surprise!

Upstairs in the dusty bedrooms
Skeletons are getting dressed
Vampires brush their hair and teeth
All the spooks must look their best!

An empty suit of shiny armour
Is clanking loudly down the hall
To a party in the ballroom
It's the monster's secret ball!

So while the party's in full swing
Be quiet as a mouse
Tiptoe out while you still can
Escape the haunted house!

Katie Mackenzie (10)
Henry Green Primary School

Grey As A Mouse

Grey as a mouse,
Big as a house,
Nose like a snake,
I make the earth shake,
As I tramp through the grass,
Trees crack as I pass,
With horns in my mouth,
I walk in the south,
Flapping big ears,
Beyond count of years,
I stump round and round,
Never lie on the ground,
Not even to die.

Yomi Adewusi (11)
Henry Green Primary School

Say 'Aagh!'

No fun being the dentist
Not much fun as a job
Spending all of your days in gazing
Right into everyone's gob

No fun seeing the dentist
Not much fun at all
Staring straight up his hairy nostrils
Drives you up the wall.

Daryl Roberts (10)
Henry Green Primary School

JUST LIKE MY DAD

Some of my friends
Want to be football stars
Some of my friends
Want to fly to the moon or Mars
Sometimes I'm good, sometimes I'm bad
But I just do my best to be just like my dad.

In my house there is lots of happiness
You'll never see any sorrow or sadness
When I'm older and get married I'm glad
I remember I just want to be just like my dad.

Darren Blackery (9)
Henry Green Primary School

AUTUMN AND WINTER

Autumn is a beautiful time
With crunchy leaves and sips of wine
Listen to the raindrops falling
Softly to the ground

Winter gives us all a shock
With turkeys, sweets and cubes of stock
The snowflakes fall swiftly down
And make our ground pure white.

Danielle Howard (10)
Henry Green Primary School

Moving

Jelly on a plate
Wibble wobble, wibble wobble
Jelly on a plate

Biscuits in a tin
Throw them up, throw them up
Biscuits in a tin

Water in a cup
Splish splosh, splish splosh
Water in a cup.

Michelle Waite (11)
Henry Green Primary School

In The Garden

In the garden where the bees fly happily
Where squirrels store their nuts for wintertime
I play happily

The birds fly rapidly in the sunny sky
I give a little sigh because I can't fly
I would touch all the birds in the sky if I could fly

The bees I see are collecting honey for me and my family
Bees are flying through the trees in the summer breeze.

Danielle Mason (9)
Henry Green Primary School

The ABC

A is for ants eating wood
B is for a ball that is in the sky
C is for a cat sleeping all day
D is for a dog barking all day
E is for an elephant eating all day
F is for a fish swimming all day
G is for giggling all day
H is for halls where people run
I is for an igloo that is so icy
J is for jam that is very sticky
K is for kangaroos jumping all day
L is for leopards running all day
M is for monkeys swinging all day
N is for noses sneezing all day
O is for octopus squiggling all day
P is for parrots talking all day
Q is for queen being smart all day
R is for Ross talking all day
S is for Sammy playing all day
T is for Tom Hocking in football
U is for umbrella keeping the rain off you
V is for violin squawking all day
W is for wine that adults drink
X is for xylophone that makes a little noise
Y is for yawning when you're tired
Z is for zebras eating all day.

Scott Ryan (9)
Hockley Primary School

Winter Snow

Winter's the season
For rain and snow
Which freezes the rivers
That used to flow

The snow's on the roof tops
The snow's on the ground
It's as white as a cloud
And it's all around.

Simon Falvey (9)
Hockley Primary School

Cows Go Moo!

Cows go moo!
Sheep go baa!
Pigs go oink!
Cockerels go mad.

Farmers go crazy
Because their farms won't shut up
So they get a hose pipe
And squirts them all up.

Cows go moo!
Sheep go baa!
Pigs go oink!
Cockerels go mad.

The farmers now
Are happy you see
Because all of their animals
Have gone away to sea.

Cows go moo!
Sheep go baa!
Pigs go oink!
Cockerels go mad.

Georgina Mann (8)
Hockley Primary School

SEASONS

S is for spring lambs and daffodils
E is for Easter eggs and chicks too
A is for autumn, fireworks and sparklers
S is for summer, sunshine's glory
O is for oranges, ripe and rich
N is for November, chilly, cold and icy
S is for snow, Santa Claus and his sleigh

Altogether it spells *seasons.*

Helen Ware (8)
Hockley Primary School

MY HAMSTER

My hamster, he is good fun
Every time we look at him he always wiggles his bum
He's got a cage, it is very big
He's got a ball, he likes to dig
When my mum tries to give him his food
He always, I mean always, bites her thumb.

Rebekah Drake (9)
Hockley Primary School

THE YAK

The yak is black
Its name is Mac,
I sit on its back
On the top of the sack,
And whack the yak
To make it clack.

Nikky Hirachan
Hockley Primary School

Snowman, Snowman

Snowman, snowman
Please don't melt
Stand in the freezer
Stand on an iceberg
Because the sun is hot
Please don't melt
Otherwise you will be
A blob on the floor
And you will be chomped
Up by the mower and
Be crunched up in the dustcart.

James Barton (9)
Hockley Primary School

My Teacher

My teacher is a nice teacher
She doesn't mind what we do
She's always busy
Doing work, of course
It is fun with my teacher
I always do what I'm asked
But I really wouldn't change her
For anyone else
No, no, no!

Sophie Sidgwick (8)
Hockley Primary School

HARVEST TIME SONG

H arvest is a time where you grow all the crops
A is for apples which is a harvest fruit
R is for resting after you have collected all the crops
V is for vegetables that people eat
E is for equipment which you cut the crops with
S is for straw which grows in the field
T is for tins which you give to other people at harvest.

Callum Druce (9)
Hockley Primary School

HARVEST

At harvest we cut the crops
So people can buy food
Such as bananas and pineapples
Peaches and apples
It is good because
We all get some fresh food
And at harvest we sing hymns.

James Hammond (8)
Hockley Primary School

THE SUN

See the sun, the sun is a star
but not here at night
It goes to a different country
so they can see the light.

Robyn Kirwan (8)
Hockley Primary School

A Frog Called Saul

There once was a frog called Saul
Who went to Hockley Primary School
He there made a big fuss
Got hit by a toy bus
And just wished he wasn't so small.

The next day he ate a big meal
To grow bigger and fat like a seal
After that he felt ill
And took a magic pill
And started rolling around like a wheel.

Then the head teacher came in and he said
Mr Frog, you should be in your bed
You've taken your pill
And look terribly ill
Then the poor little fellow dropped dead!

Gemma Ford (9)
Hockley Primary School

Dolphins, Dolphins, Dolphins

Dolphins are always smiling, smiling, smiling
The dolphin photos are piling, piling, piling
Even though they're grey and love the sun, sun, sun
They're still really, really fun, fun, fun.

Dolphins shouldn't be endangered species, species, species
People use their blubber for different bits and pieces
I think people who kill dolphins should be ashamed of themselves.

Kerry Lawrence (11)
Hockley Primary School

CANDLE

My candle
flickers in
the night.
Makes my
bedroom very
bright. When
I look at it
my candle,
no more
flickers.
It's not
very bright.

Sheldon Cooper (10)
Hockley Primary School

FIREWORK

I'm a firework
Shooting up to the sky
Boom!
Goes my gunpowder
Exploding in the sky
Wow!
Says my audience
The other fireworks are racing
And I win the race.

Sean Petley (9)
Hockley Primary School

THE WHOLE OF CHRISTMAS

Slippery snowman
Nowhere to go
On the ground is frost and snow
Everyone knows winter's on its way
Throwing snowballs, everyone's laughing
Through the tiptoeing snow
After that, father's in the kitchen doing a bit of that
Everyone is having fun cleaning up the kitchen
with their mop and sponge
Friends and family opening presents
Oops, I almost forgot the cake then we try and sing
I really do see the point of Christmas.

Robert Duffill (8)
Hockley Primary School

MY HOT FOOT

My hot foot is very hot
I cannot
bear it,
I blow it
and put it in a bucket of cold water
I hate putting it in the fridge
Maybe I can go back to sleep
Zzzz!
Oh no! Now I've got a cold foot.

Sam Pruden (8)
Hockley Primary School

MARK GALLOTT TALKALOT

There is a boy in our class called
Mark Gallott Talkalot
He sits in class and talks all day
And only stops when he's all talked out
He never finishes his work and always gets told off
And that's why he's called
Mark Gallott Talkalot.

Mark Gallott (9)
Hockley Primary School

SPACE

Space . . .
Stars shooting,
Asteroids somersaulting
Spinning planets
Black holes sucking
Twirling satellites
Fuming rockets
Boiling sun
Red-hot Mars
Icy Pluto
Giant Jupiter
Orbiting Venus
Saturn with its rings
Blue Neptune
Living Earth
Galactic Uranus
Martian-infested Mercury
Space, the final frontier.

Charlotte Sabbarton (10)
Riverside CJ School

Loneliness

I wander around,
Nowhere to go,
No one to talk to
No one I know.

This is torture,
It's unreal,
There's only one escape from this,
Death!

The ground is littered with dead corpses,
When will it end?
When will it end?
I ask myself each day.

Then suddenly, out of the darkness,
Comes a glimmer of light,
Maybe there is hope,
Then I could escape this dreadful place.

Matthew Gilmore (11)
Riverside CJ School

The Miserable Duck

The miserable duck,
He always clucks,
Sometimes he is fond,
Of the green and white pond,
He's always in front of the dinner line,
To get some lovely red wine,
So he should be in front of the miserable queue,
Then he will be one of few.

Natalie Frith (11)
Riverside CJ School

GOING A-CREEPING

Rusty gates
Creaky door
Rickety stairs
I'm really scared.

Bumping shutters
Flying sheets
Bloody puddles
Groaning tree.

Moaning wind
Tail-less cat.

Headless horseman
Marching zombies.

Howling chimney
Warty toad
Piercing shriek
Melting grave.
Aaaarrrhhh!

Lucy Hollington (9)
Riverside CJ School

OUR SOLAR SYSTEM

Somewhere in the universe
Our solar system lies,
Nine planets with countless moons
Orbit around the sun.

Black holes and comets
Sometimes are a worry,
Some crash into planets
And then cause disaster.

All these things together
Make up our solar system,
All of these are active
Twenty-four hours a day.

Megan Barrett (10)
Riverside CJ School

MINI MARTIAN VISIT

Snuggled up in bed
I cuddle my Ted,
I am full of fright
As someone turns on the light.
A mini Martian has come to visit me
Help! I think he is going to eat me for his tea!

He has travelled from space.
With a big red suitcase,
I think he comes from Mars,
But he eats loads of Milky Way bars,
He is wriggling his fifteen toes
And he has a twitchy long nose.

He approaches my bed with a curious smile,
Oh how I wish I could run a whole mile.
Through a gap in the curtains he catches the sight,
Of the twinkling stars and the bright moonlight.
This makes him think of his family far away,
And the fun and games he used to play.

With a crash and a bang he makes for the sky,
With a wave and a smile he squeaks '*goodbyeeee.*'

Charlotte Gilmore (9)
Riverside CJ School

Laser Beams

Quick aliens
Robots shoot
Aliens shrivel
Demons come out of a spaceship
Demons throw gas bombs
They have laser beams
The have terrifying *explosions.*
Frightening demons
Go back in their spaceship and
Shoot through tunnels.

Ben Taylor Edwards (9)
Riverside CJ School

War

Horrifying guns fire bullets
Red blood splattered everywhere
Ghastly soldiers lose badges
Rockets blow up base
Germans want revenge.

Danny Henry (8)
Riverside CJ School

The Redbreasted Robin

There stepped the rich redbreasted robin.
Stepping majestically on the crispy glistening snow in front of the sun.
'*Wow!*' said the little boy 'I've never seen one of those,
It's a magical redbreasted robin.

It's stepping up a hollow, glistening white tree
I can see.
Then I see another rich redbreasted robin.
I think robins are the best.'

Matthew Dendle (11)
Riverside CJ School

An Eagle

He clings on the rocks with his crooked hands,
Close to the moon in the lonely lands,
Looking down upon the misty sky he stands.

The wrinkled sea beneath him crawls,
He watches from the mountain, as he cools,
And like a thunderbolt he falls.

Tom Frith (11)
Riverside CJ School

Ninja

A battle of steel
He has fallen
He can remember his defeat
As he is carried home by a passing traveller.

His sword shattered
He has lost his honour
He is ashamed
Next battle, he will die
He hopes his clan will live forever.

Adam Wesley (10)
Riverside CJ School

TIGRESS

Padding quietly through the forest,
Searching for her prey,
Going hungry
For another day,
Coming back to her cubs,
They start to whimper and cry,
Then they start to play again the tigress wonders why
Early morning,
The tigress pads outside
Her eyes are blazing red
And full of pride.
The tigress hears some hooves
Padding on the ground
She sees a deer and
Makes no sound.
She hides behind an overgrown bush
The deer walks past to graze
The tigress pounces on him as fast as lightning
The tigress's eyes yet again turn a red blaze.
The tigress
Drags the deer back
To her cubs
They cry with glee when they see the tasty snack.
The cubs dream,
To be like their mother
And then they,
Snuggle up against another.

Kayleigh Streeter (10)
Riverside CJ School

Motherless Child

Is it necessary to put her on the streets?
Homeless, mum-less, dad-less! Nowhere to live!
Please help her!
She must be bitterly cold,
Her fingertips must be icicles.
Hair not brushed, tangled like fishing nets together.

No one wants her!
She wants to be taken away and cared for
She wants a mum and dad
Just like her old mum and dad.
She is starving like an animal
She is ill as if she was poisoned
She is digging for her hungry life.
Please help her!

Jemma Burrell (11)
Riverside CJ School

What Lies Up There

As I walk out into the garden on a cold frosty night,
I stare at the moonlit sky and wonder what lies up there,
Maybe a magical planet mystical and colourful,
Or a shooting star whizzing across the sky.

I wish I could visit this enchanting place,
And explore my own magical planet,
To answer the question that no one has before.
What lies up there?

Tom Bottrill (11)
Riverside CJ School

A Martian On A Meteor

A Martian on a meteor crashed down to Earth one day,
It landed in my garden, maybe it wanted to play!
I went and got my telescope to look for shooting stars,
He started crying and told me he could see his home on Mars.
I asked the Martian into my house for a cup of tea,
I'm not sure if he understood, but he followed nervously,
I made him a new spaceship to send him through the atmosphere,
The Martian touched me on the nose and shot off with a cheer.
Am I talking to a Martian, is it really true?
I can't believe I'm doing this . . . do you?

Charlotte Williamson (9)
Riverside CJ School

Rise Of The Devil

Walking through the forest
Sun goes down,
Moon comes up
Night falls in the forest.
A bit of red light and the ground bursts open!
A devil comes to.
Fire rages through the forest,
Heard a scream, blood and guts fly.

Jamie Kennedy (8)
Riverside CJ School

Fitness

Fitness is good for you
Fitness helps your heart,
If you don't do it,
It could hurt your heart.

Fitness is good,
It's fun to do,
It makes your blood,
Flow strong and true.

Jenni-Ann Davis (11)
Riverside CJ School

I'm Excited

I'm excited and I don't know why,
My friends are coming over
For some tea,
That's what my mum told me.
It's going to be great
Come on! My friends are going to be here soon
'They're here!'
Yeah!
It's my birthday.

Rachel Wheate (10)
Riverside CJ School

Martian

My brother had a strange look on his face,
He'd seen a Martian from outer space.
There was something that puzzled me
I thought Martians were a fantasy.
I rubbed my eyes in disbelief,
It had one eye and goofy teeth!
It had a plump belly and it was green,
It's the most amazing thing I have ever seen.

Charlie Gradon (9)
Riverside CJ School

My Rabbit George

My rabbit George
Is my best friend,
He looks forward
To when I come home.
He always likes lots of cuddles,
He sits in his hutch all day
Eating a carrot
And drinking water.
George loves me and I love George.

James Hyde (11)
Riverside CJ School

Zombies And Devils Arise With The Giants

Dead zombies arise with the devils
And the giants are all coming towards us.
Destructive and terribly frightening.
The horned devils coming to the north,
The stomping giants coming to the east.
The green blood zombies coming to the south
And all their babies to the west.
Will this be the end of people? Who knows!
Haahaahaa!

David Jellett (8)
Riverside CJ School

Dancing Meteorites

Massive meteorites
Are fast and funky
They think they're cool
But are really crazy.

They go to discos and
Have loud music,
And no one can stop them
They're so hard and dancy.

Gary Wheate (9)
Riverside CJ School

MY LIFE AS A FOOTBALL

Ouch! Eeek! That hurt!
I'm covered in mud
I'm being kicked.
What shall I do?
I'll be taken away
By the man of the match,
Oh no, here he comes,
Farewell!

Luke Wilson (11)
Riverside CJ School

THE FLASH OF STEEL

The flash of steel,
The birth of cold,
He has experienced the seven worlds,
Do eyes remain in this drifting world?

Life in darkness, death in defeat,
Horrid disgrace to his clan.
He no longer needs his sword
As the evening wind will carry him home.

Luke Bosdet (11)
Riverside CJ School

Sunrise

I step into the morning,
I feel it wash over me
Like a fresh breeze on a summer's day
I drink in the sweet scent of dewdrops,
glistening on the crisp grass
I hear the twittering of birds,
gathering food,
feeding their young
I look into the sunrise;
glinting red;
the horizon hiding the full view of magnificence itself
I understand the elegance
people are unaware of the beauty it conceals.

Maria Cansella (11)
Riverside CJ School

Seasons

Winter's cold
Summer goes,
Autumn falls
Spring calls.

Spring, summer, autumn and winter,
Are our four seasons.

When it's snowing,
Snowflakes are falling,
I hear someone calling
It's the winter robin.

Abbie Gilbert (11)
Riverside CJ School

LIFE AS A CAT

Life as a cat is lazy,
Life as a cat is cosy.
Cats are lucky
They're very cuddly.

They are very active,
Very fantastic,
They like fish
Out of a dish.

They like mice,
They think they're so nice.
Outside is fun,
Why don't you come?
Miaow!

Sheree Gillingham
Riverside CJ School

THE LION

In Africa where he lay waiting for his prey
Roaarr!
Swishing his tail
Licking his lips
He sees a gazelle, jumps to his feet
The chase begins
The lion has won, until the next time.

Matthew Linton (11)
Riverside CJ School

A Moonlit Sea

Among the silver-lit stars
Lay beneath
A moonlit sea

Calm, gentle
Swaying from edge to edge
Glistening.

As the moon shines
Upon the sea
Brightly.

Sparkling in the sun
Admiring its glaze
A moonlit sea.

Jessie Moye (10)
Riverside CJ School

Football

Goal! Goal!
The commentator screams,
Fans go wild and jump off their seats,
The referee blows the whistle
They've won again.
They're on a winning streak,
Cameras flash, children scream
But the battle lives on!

Matthew Lloyd (11)
Riverside CJ School

The Clouds

The clouds are fluffy,
They follow you to most places,
They crash, they join
They swirl around, dancing like fairies
Beneath you hear splashing rain as you go.
Clouds change shape in many different ways
Beneath you hear splashing rain as you go,
They swirl around, dancing like fairies
They crash, they join,
They follow you to most places,
The clouds are fluffy.

Amelia Chambers (10)
Riverside CJ School

Shadows

Mystical creatures flying way up high,
Shapes and shadows, legends that lie,
Horses with horns and reptiles that fly.

Magic writings ripped and torn,
Colossal dragons set fire to corn,
Beautiful lands decrepit and forlorn.

All these shadows soar through the night,
Roaring with colours so bright.

Charlotte Ball (10)
Riverside CJ School

COME FLY WITH ME

I see the stars and moon at night,
There're lots of planets out of sight.
The Bear, the Plough and Milky Way too,
All there as well to be looked at by you.
A shooting star is lucky to see
So make a wish and come fly with me.

Kirsty Burkett (10)
Riverside CJ School

ANGRY GIANTS

Tremendous, dangerous, angry giants.
Blatantly evil and very mean.
People get squashed, things smash
And blood flies everywhere.

Then silence all over the land.

Craig Bliss (9)
Riverside CJ School

BLUE IS . . .

Blue is my favourite colour,
Blue is as magnificent as the atmosphere of the sky.
Blue is as dark as the relaxing winter sky
Blue is as light as the tropical ocean.
Blue is the colour of the glistening ice,
Blue is my favourite colour.

Bradley Baker (10)
Riverside CJ School

The Martian And Satanian

The Martian and Satanian went to space
in a supersonic ship,
They took some red stuff and plenty of green stuff
wrapped up in a galactic button.
The aliens looked up at the shooting stars
and started to sing,
'We're heading for Mars, we are, we are, we are,
We're heading for Mars we are!'
They orbited the stars for a light year and a zap
towards the mountainous black hole,
And there on a crater an astronaut did stand with the
moon on the palm of his hand.
'Dear astronaut are you borg to give up your moon
for a Zorg?'
'My moon,' said the astronaut, 'I will,'
Then they zapped away on their holiday,
around the Milky Way.

'Over and out.'

Coral Richardson (9)
Riverside CJ School

Tiger Eyes

Eyes as bright as the moonlight,
Prowling through the forest of the night
As if he was the king of the world
All powerful.
The animals are his servants,
The penalty
Look into my eyes.

Lauren Warner (11)
Riverside CJ School

SECRET PASSAGES

In quiet, dark passages,
The snow falls, raining heavily
When suddenly a door opens.
Long paths
Quick, quiet running.

Creepy curves,
Turning and swerving
Different footprints are going places
Far, far away through the passages
Further than the Earth's limit . . .

New paths are opened,
More turning
And soon after,
All the snow passages slowly disappear
Fading, fading faster.

Gone!

Luke Fisher (9)
Riverside CJ School

THE ZOMBIE STRIKES BACK!

Lightning *strikes!*

Everyone knows it's the night of the *zombie!*
The zombie gets out of its grave
The zombie howls till midnight
The people are guarding their children
Screams fill the air
Someone has been *executed!*

Billy Radmore (9)
Riverside CJ School

ON THE WAY UP TO SPACE

On the way up to space
In the rocket there is a place
We will travel at a fast pace
On the way up to space.

On the way up to space
The stars shine bright and give us light
The moon is near, we're nearly there
On the way up to space.

On the way up to space
I saw an alien dressed in lace
Dancing and singing with great taste
On the way up to space.

Now it's time for me to go
In the rocket with a fresh glow
The moon was fun but now I'm done
So home to bed, my poem is done.

April Williams (10)
Riverside CJ School

PET FRIENDS

Rabbits are small with lopped ears,
Kittens are soft, which dry your tears.
Dogs protect you with all their might
Guinea pigs are cute, so hug them tight!
Budgies are companions for your life,
Rats have claws as sharp as a knife!
All the animals around the world
Are good friends, as I have told.

Michaela Buckley (10)
Riverside CJ School

Destroy Space

Dark gloomy planets
Scary aliens emerge from the moon.
Lasers murder
Dirty blood
Spaceship explosion
Death
Dangerous bombs.
Bang!

Emily Brewer (8)
Riverside CJ School

Secret Passages

Scary!
Black, dark, twisty turning tunnels,
Horrible ghosts in black holes.
Spooky doors,
Creep, creepy crawlies.
Scream!

Rebecca Hall (8)
Riverside CJ School

Devils Rise

Devils rise with lots of spooky noises
Going on the floor with beastly noises.
Ghosts groaning down in the cellar,
Devils ask for revenge . . .
Aaghh!

Jennie Wells (9)
Riverside CJ School

WHAT'S OUT THERE?

Motionless
I stand gazing up at the sky,
Wondering if any life is out there
What's that?
Oh just another star
I'll never find anything.

Kaboooom!
Wow! That must be real,
I've finally found something!
Wait until my friends find out about this!

Callum Ginbey (10)
Riverside CJ School

ALIENS' WAR

Lasers kill and destroy
Purple blood flying
People have died.
Aliens get revenge
Weapons are killing
Aliens kill
And
Aliens slaughter
Aliens destroy
Aliens execute
We failed the war.

Jo Mead (9)
Riverside CJ School

DEVILS RISE

Huge, horned, evil devils rise up
They set the creepy forest on fire!
They fly all around the city and scare everyone,
All the people were horrified . . . they ran!
Everyone screamed.
Haaoouu!
A ghost hunter went to the devil's territory,
A very creepy, very dark night.
Fear, noises,
Devils surrounded him silently.
No one ever knew what they did to him.
Did they eat him?
Was he their prisoner forever?

David Worrow (8)
Riverside CJ School

THE MILLENNIUM

M any years have passed
I have only lived for ten
L et this day
L ight up the party time
E njoy the food and drinks,
N ow it's time to celebrate
N ever again will this time be here
I n my lifetime
U p in the sky we see the sign '2000'
M ay this be the day of my lifetime.

Martin Harrild (10)
Riverside CJ School

Our Hamster

Our hamster called Twinkle
Rustles around her cage at night,
Runs around her wheel
She is a funny sight.
Every night she's in her ball
She comes close when we call.
Her food she likes to keep in her cheeks
Thinking it will last for weeks.
At the end of each night she feels worn out
Time for bed, no more running about.
Curled up tight, feeling nice and hot
Dreaming of all the food that she has got.

Lilli Weekley (8)
Riverside CJ School

The Lady Of Winter

The lady of winter comes from the sky in her
dresses of pearls and diamonds, she glitters.
The holly berries are her red rosy cheeks,
Her long blonde hair is the bright sun on the
fresh white snow of her face.
Winter is nearly over now, the lady of winter is
getting ready to hibernate for the New Year,
Whilst the lady of spring is getting ready to
create the new season.

Jade Whitelock (10)
Riverside CJ School

ZOMBIES, GHOSTS AND GHOULS

Ghosts, ghouls rise
Zombies haunt creepy graveyards
Strange language.
Walk, crunch,
Twigs, leaves.
Open the coffin
Curse!
Nasty scary zombies, ghosts, ghouls.
Kill him!

Aaaggghh!

Kathleen Cochrane (8)
Riverside CJ School

A DEVIL'S DAY OUT!

Devils rise. Smoke rises
Destroy, kill and die.
People stabbed to death
Lance and kill the humans, eat the meat.
A membrane of dead humans
A blood box!
The humans are terrified,
A sword comes out of the sky and kills the devils.
The devils die
Yellow blood.

Matthew Smith (8)
Riverside CJ School

My Poem

This is my spell for Hallowe'en night
If it works you'll get a fright.

Eye of dog and rabbit's paw,
One dead frog and an apple core,
Put them in the pot and light the fire
Watch them melt as the flames get alight,
Add some blood and a bogey too
And if you can find one, a smelly old shoe.
Stir it up with an eagle's claw
And it will turn into a mother-in-law.

This is spell number two:
I'm not quite sure just what to do.
I'll make my brew and say my spell
I'm not sure it will work, as you can tell.
If I get the mixture right
Then I'm sure you'll get a fright.
I could create a hairy creature
Or maybe even a scary teacher.

Casey Hamill (9)
St Katherine's CE Primary School, Canvey Island

Soldiers

Sent out to fight
Others safe holding on tight
Looking sorrowfully while they hope
Demolished houses held up by rope.
In those fields poppies grew
Exchanged gifts rare but true
Red blood in poppy fields
Soldiers holding up their shields.

Laura Olley (10)
St Katherine's CE Primary School, Canvey Island

Our School Netball Match

I like playing netball, I think it is cool
And I look super when I've got the ball.
I jump high to take my shot
I try and try, but miss a lot
When I'm steady, I take a fling,
And watch the ball fly through the ring.
I run so fast, I slip and slide
If I'm not careful, I'll be offside.
When we are good and make a catch
This can lead to winning our match.
After we've won, we clap and cheer
And look forward to playing next year.

Daina Peters (10)
St Katherine's CE Primary School, Canvey Island

I Think About My Father

I think about my father
Almost every day
I think about my father
When I go to school and play
I often ask my mother
To take me to his grave
So that I may remember
That my father was brave

My father was a soldier
In the Second World War
And each day I think of him
I love him even more.

Elizabeth Davies (10)
St Katherine's CE Primary School, Canvey Island

SOLDIER

Soldier, soldier, where am I
Is our food, cold mince pie?
I really want to have a roast
Every time you have a slice of toast.
Do we get a mailman knocking at our door?
Do we have mice running around the floor?
Will there be girls in another hut?
Are we roasting roasted nuts?
Are we doing any of those
No! Wake up you sleepy head,
You're still in your pantihose.

Rhea Varker (9)
St Katherine's CE Primary School, Canvey Island

A LIVING NIGHTMARE!

As the ghost floats through the air
Filling me with awful scare.
It can't be a ghost. I mention,
Or could it be? I question.

As the ghoul floats up the stair
Filling me with awful scare.
As the zombie weirdly walks
And the dracula horribly stalks.

I suddenly jump with an almighty *scream!*
Never mind it was only a dream!

Molly Collisson (10)
St Katherine's CE Primary School, Canvey Island

JAZMIN

My cousin Jazmin has just been born,
She's really sweet and cuddly
When she's wrapped up in her shawl.
She's got a small chubby face
And a button nose,
Small little legs and
Bright pink toes.

My cousin Jazmin has just turned one,
Even though she's really little
It feels like she weighs a ton.
She's up to my shoulder
She's really, really tall.
And when I stand next to her
It makes me feel like a fool.

My cousin Jazmin is a really cheeky pest.
She runs around the house all day
In her knickers and her vest.
She never stops to breathe
She's always being mad
And when no one comes to see her
It makes her really sad.

Rachel Louise Hurley (10)
St Katherine's CE Primary School, Canvey Island

SWIM LIKE MAD

Bang! The gun goes
I want to win.
Splash! Goes the water as the people dive in.
Bang! I hear the gun go off again.
It's a false start in one of the lanes.
I stop swimming, turn and check it's not me,
But the judge is pointing to a girl in lane three.
We climb on the blocks and wait for the start.
I can hear lots of thumping,
I think it's my heart.
We're off once again
And we're swimming like mad.
'Go for it Sophie!'
Shouts my dad.
I can see the end of the pool coming up,
And I can imagine myself holding a big silver cup.
As I think that I have won the race,
I realise I've finished in sixth place.
No silver cup
I got beaten by the rest
But at least I know, I've done my best.

Sophie Kneeshaw (10)
St Katherine's CE Primary School, Canvey Island

HALLOWE'EN

Hallowe'en is eerie and dark
Goblins, witches in the park
Waiting for the children at night
Waiting to give them a scary fright

Trick or treaters stroll the towns
In wicked masks and fairy gowns
Hoping they'll get lots of sweets
Chocolate bars and bon-bon treats

Witches cackling in the caves
Rising dead from the graves
Mixing spiders, toads and snails
And a pinch of doggy tails

Phantoms white as white can be
Floating by so peacefully
The people are asleep it seems
They haunt the people in their dreams

Dracular gives us a scare
Biting people here and there
Turning into vicious bats
Drawing blood from mice and rats

The clock strikes twelve, ding-dong
Hallowe'en has been and gone
Lots of people waiting keen
For the next year's Hallowe'en.

Bobbie Barrett (10)
St Katherine's CE Primary School, Canvey Island

My Nan And Grandad Brown

My nan and grandad Brown
always go to the town.

They eat lots of food,
which puts them in a good mood.

My grandad likes doing crosswords
my nan always feeds the birds.

My nan has got a sewing machine,
my grandad has got a scooter that everyone has seen.

My grandad likes to look at maps,
and also likes to take short naps.

My nan's real name is Maud,
but that is not what she likes to be called.

They live together
so they're not on they're own
it's a really lovely and cosy home.

They've got a nice carpet
which they got from the market.

They've got two sheds,
and quite a few beds.

They've got nice neighbours,
who do them lots of favours.

And that's the true poem about my
nan and grandad Brown.

Theresa Nunn (10)
St Katherine's CE Primary School, Canvey Island

BRUNO

I have a little bunny
Bruno is his name,
He's brown and white and fluffy
And his ears don't look the same.
One flops down and looks so cute
The other stands up tall.
But I don't care what he looks like
He's the best bunny of them all.

Emma Burch (9)
St Katherine's CE Primary School, Canvey Island

DON'T BLAME ME!

My dad says this word all the time
He says it means grown up.
Responsibility he mentions
He said I lack it a lot.

When things go wrong I'm liable
My sister's in the clear.
It's me who takes the blame for things
Because it's me who's always near.

My mum says I'm always naughty
That I don't behave at all.
She thinks she's always right
Since she's so big and I'm so small.

Everything's always my fault
I'm always to blame you see.
I try to do everything right
So please please don't blame me!

Natalie Mohile (11)
Stifford Primary School

OLD MRS BROWN

Old Mrs Brown who teaches Class 2
Has blue eyes and curly brown hair
As well as some wrinkles
She has lots of pimples
And a horrible nasty stare.

Old Mrs Brown who teaches Class 2
Is someone you need to avoid
If your maths book's a sight
And your answers aren't right
She's bound to be very annoyed.

Old Mrs Brown who teaches Class 2
Cannot stand disrespect and noise
Her particular hate
Is if someone is late
(And that's usually one of the boys)

Old Mrs Brown who teaches Class 2
Always makes maths homework boring
It is her intention
To set me detention
That instantly sends me snoring.

Old Mrs Brown who teaches Class 2
Has some sort of thing against me
She just cannot abide
That I just can't divide
But that's how it will always be.

Old Mrs Brown who teaches Class 2
Is certainly quite a preacher
She should be a vicar
As she tends to bicker
But she'll do as my maths teacher.

Clare Rowland (10)
Stifford Primary School

THE SHIPWRECK

Among the gusty seas
A ribbon moonlight path,
We see it lying there
At the bottom of the ocean.
People passed over it
There it still lies in the ocean
Its windows lay there shattered
Whilst it lay in pieces.
Which was pitiful, it killed many lives
The shipwreck lay there,
Like a sleepy dog on the highway
Whilst above the wind twisted and
Twirled like a tornado building up
Its unstoppable strength.
For its next journey.
It lay unstoppable, breathing deep
Inside its depth it was dark, dank and dreary.
Building up his piece from the strength of the tornado.
Now the ship's strength was as strong as a gorilla.
However this journey wasn't over.

Sean Doyle & Daniel McDonald (11)
Thames View Junior School

PUPPETS

'Why is it called the Theatre Museum Miss?
Why is it a museum?
What is it used for Miss?
Why are they full of puppets?

Why are puppets made from rubber Miss?
Why are they called puppets?
Why do they wear clothes Miss?
Why are they in the museum?

Why are there shadow puppets Miss?
Why are puppets big?
When were puppets first made Miss?
Why was rubber a good material for them?

Who thought of the name puppet Miss?
Why are puppets funny?
Why are puppets in the Theatre Museum Miss?
Why are they made to play with?'

Bola Bademosi (10)
Thames View Junior School

THE DEEP DARK SEA

The huge waves shattered,
they shattered into raindrops
like a glass breaking.

The naked trees watched
as the leaves of autumn fell
they watched in despair.

The high cliffs crumbled,
they crumbled down like breadcrumbs
and fell into the swirling vortex.

Colossal black clouds
looked down at the angered sea,
and shouted a deep shout.

The two forces screamed
they went head to head, they fought.
The wind won and the sea settled.
The silence was so unexpected, so unnatural.

Jodie Savill (11)
Thames View Junior School

THE PLANETS

All nine planets orbiting the giant
shining sun, in the world of space.

With asteroids and comets passing by to
its destination, where would it die?

As you go further you'll get lonelier
but as you go further it'll be darker.

Passing the spinning planets,
Jupiter, Saturn . . . who knows where you'll go.
Maybe in a black hole!

The jungle
Jaguars skidding round the corners
of the jungle.

Pumas racing cheetahs along the rivers
of the jungle.

Poison snakes slivering, twisting,
turning around your body.

Squeezing your neck until you go pale.

Sohail Qureshi (11)
Thames View Junior School

JUNGLE

Vines swinging everywhere,
Falcons flying through the air,
Eagles swooping down to their prey
Snakes laying waiting for their prey.

Monkeys swinging from vine to vine,
Gorillas swinging, breaking every vine,
Little lime lizard tasting the air with his fork-like tongue,
Cheaters are running, not being so fair.

Elephants stampeding through the green,
Lions roaring, feeling keen.
Tigers eating, flashing off their stripes.
Savages, savages, savages.

Debo Adekoluejo (11)
Thames View Junior School

RAINBOW COLOURS

Red is a beautiful rose
growing in a lovely flower garden,
Or sweet tasty blood
coming from my arm.

Blue is the sparkling sea
from the beach water,
Or the beautiful blue sky
where the birds fly.

Yellow is the lovely golden sun
shining over the school playground,
Or a yellow book
at our school.

Pink is a pair of lips
Shining in the sun,
Or a pink pen
on my desk.

Green is fresh grass
in our school field,
Or a green pencil
which I write with.

Victoria Downes (10)
Thames View Junior School

As I Peer Through My Marble . . .

As I peer through my spacious marble,
I see . . .
the ocean waves fiercely
splashing with a soft white
a rough blue
a funky green.
the colours mixed together are a . . .
horrible dripping sea monster
coming out of the sea.

As I gaze through my glassy marble,
I see . . .
my classroom, everybody listening
light blues, dark greys
clear whites and scary blacks
all the colours look like . . .
the summer's day
and the wintry nights.

As I glimpse through my smooth marble,
I see . . .
a cosy cottage standing
with funny cows and woolly sheep
all the colours look like my messy bedroom curtains.

As I gaze through my mysterious marble,
I see . . .
a fire-breathing hungry
dragon dancing and prancing
with a young fighter called Bianca,
all the fierce reds and frightening yellows
remind me of barley sugar sweets
melting in my mouth.

Adelaide Aloto (10)
Thames View Junior School

A World In A Marble

As I gaze into my marble I see

Waves, huge waves
crashing against the
seabed.

Dolphin, blue dolphins
jumping in the cool sea
flipping and diving around.

Fun, brilliant fun
when I look into
my marble and
see things that's fun.

Seeing, blissful seeing
I see in my marble
A world, a different
world made out of
colours and glass.

Bubble, a smooth clear bubble
is the shape of my
shy marble.

Inside, deep inside
I see swirling colours
around and around.

Lush blue
Sparkly yellow
Dangerous red
Grass green
That's my marble.

Daisy Brand (9)
Thames View Junior School

COLOUR

Red is the colour of roses shining
in the sun
or a lovely dress at a party ball.

Blue is the colour of a beautiful sea
flowing on the sandy beach
or a bright sunny sky
in the summer day.

Gold is the colour of glitter lights
in the glittery disco
or a shining gold coin in the treasure box.

White is the colour of fluffy clouds
making funny shapes while I'm laying down
or a clean white sheet of pupils are drawing on.

Nurul Shawal (9)
Thames View Junior School

THE STORM

The moon was a ghastly galleon as it
lit up the cloudy sky
The sky was like a thick black,
velvety blanket.
The wind was a torrent of darkness,
whistling throughout the naked trees.
Raindrops fell like darts aiming
for a bullseye.
The waves crashed against the rocks like
lions roaring, trying to escape a cage.

Carly Prince (11)
Thames View Junior School

The Sun

The blazing sun
struck the aquamarine sea,
It twisted, twirled and
turned in the air it
was waiting to pounce.
One look at it and I knew
I was its next victim.

Nicky Moir (10)
Thames View Junior School

Leaves

Twisting, twirling, turning
Through the air.
Like a pleasant, elegant ballerina
Gliding across the floor.
Then the fragile leaves delicately
Flew to a corner to relax.

Mary Sparrow (11)
Thames View Junior School

The Voyage

Hot, tired, bothered
Bored as I watched cars speed past,
Excited, for I was going on holiday,
As hot as the fireball shone on to the car.
Travelling is boring, but exciting.

Emma Gentry-Moore (10)
Thames View Junior School

SAD

Sad, sad
Under a wet dirty cloth
Dark, dark
As I lay in my loft
Hope, hope
I had some light up here
Wish, wish
I had a better home than this

Wish, wish
Some luck would come my way
Otherwise I'll have to pack
My bags and go away
Some day.

Adam John McCarthy (9)
Thames View Junior School

SPIDERS

Spiders, spiders
Creepy crawly, dark and small
Slowly walking, chills you with fright
Makes you chatter, ends with a fright

Spiders, spiders
Crawling up the wall
Scared I am, but with all my might
I hold my teeth tight.

Harrish Santron (10)
Thames View Junior School

The Unknown Sun

This sun is bright
This sun is sharp
Cutting through your blazed heart.

This sun is shining through the day,
Cover your face,
And make sure not to get burned.

Eliminating shadows,
Slaughtering prey,
Always seen in the light of day.

Waiting for people
Staying at bay
Never seen in the unknown grey.

He strikes at once
With amazing speed
Only when your heart is full of fear.

Jonathan Hamza-Amalou & Danil Nevsky (11)
Thames View Junior School

The Loner

She sits by the rocks searching, staring, sighing
Every day still there.
Not a wink
Not a smile
Always late for class
Tapping her hands against the rock,
Her feet copying the shadows of the children
Playing with excitement.

Robert Owen (11)
Thames View Junior School

The Cave

The cave, dark, dank and dreary,
Sharp objects stand, ferocious,
Cutting anyone's legs to ribbons
Blood lies in a puddle on the floor.

Black bears lurking around
They sniff, sniff, sniff, sniff, sniff.
They smell the faintest smell,
Tracking their prey, they snap at them.

We get to the core
We slip, slither, slide around.
The crumbling ice cracks
We stumbled
'Ahhhh!'

Jason Fuller (11)
Thames View Junior School

The Castle

The castle was a shadow in the
distance, gazing upon us,
Its walls were covered with moss,
The windows were cobwebbed so badly
they looked like cracked icing on a cake.

We opened the great oak door,
cascading dust fell upon us.
Cobwebs were strangling vases,
standing statues stood proud, like soldiers.
Gargoyle's heads with blazing red eyes.

Charlie Graham (11) & Louis Ginn (10)
Thames View Junior School

The Poor Pig

Poor pig
Poor pig
What's it like to wear a wig?

Poor pig
Poor pig
How far can you really dig?

Poor pig,
Poor pig,
Do you ever go anywhere?

Poor pig,
Poor pig
Do you really have any hair?

Davern Olivacce (10)
Thames View Junior School

Lost

Lost, lost
Lost on a caravan site.

Scared, scared
Waiting for someone to find me.

Crying, crying
Tears trickling down my face, endlessly.

Hope, hope
God, please help me find my mum and dad.

Danielle Peaty (11)
Thames View Junior School

ALONE

Alone
Alone
As I get left in the dark,
I'm all on my own.

Waiting
Waiting
While I wait in the dark
For someone to come.

Bored
Bored
There's nothing to do
I'm asking you.

Cheer
Cheer
I'm glad
Someone's here.

Caroline Head (11)
Thames View Junior School

THE STORM

The effects on land were devastating
Not a mortal moved, nor a plant.
Twisting, twirling there was no peace around
Winds blew majestically, like a prince on horseback,
Leaves twisting and twirling, like a kite out of control,
Engrossed in the atmosphere, we stood
Knowing what was coming . . . hair on end.

Tola Odedoyin (11)
Thames View Junior School

The Storm

It was deadly quiet
Not a leaf rustled,
Nor a rat squeaked
In this small village.
A swift shower of rain fell
Like some urgent messenger - rush of wind.
The deadly hurricane which was a twisting, twirling whirlpool,
Ripped its way through that village, that same small village.
The wind was as rapid as a diver plunging down the side of a cliff,
The waves crashed against the rocks like fierce lions hunting for prey.
The merciless and unstoppable hurricane died down for a while
Again it went back to that quiet, that unnatural quiet.
The village was left as a scrapyard, for the time being.

Ewan Macaulay (11)
Thames View Junior School

The Storm

Winds were like fierce lions chasing their prey
round and round dark corners,
cutting and ripping their way through the dark streets.

Winds were twisting and twirling in the midnight sky.

Slamming and whistling as it tore zinc sheets
off of rooftops.

Twisting and twirling them like bits of rubber.

The sea twisted and turned as it slammed endlessly
against the worn out rocky cliffs.

Steven Deller (11)
Thames View Junior School

THE SUN

Hot, hot the blazing
sun looked down
at me.

Sweat, sweat as the
sweat dropped down
off me.

Clouds, clouds were
as frothy as froth
on a cappuccino
which covered the sun.

Sun, sun was like
a red-hot fireball
rising through the
azure blue sky.

Sarah Cullen & Sarah Brown (10)
Thames View Junior School

THE THEATRE MUSEUM

Puppets, puppets everywhere
I liked it when I got there.
Magician, magician, played with a balloon.
Went to give it to a boy but it shot around the room.
Cold, cold, it was inside.
Under my clothes I tried to hide.
Forkbeard's, Forkbeard's Exhibition
Running around like on a mission.

Danny Buckhorn (10)
Thames View Junior School

PLAIN OLD WEEK

First it's Monday
No! School again!
Such a shame!

Tuesday looks all right . . .
but . . . *Oh no!* There's a fight!

Wednesday it's getting better . . .
but it's also getting wetter.

Thursday. Yes okay!
Just one more day!

Friday, tomorrow's the day!
Home time. Hip hip hooray!

Saturday, relaxing, holiday.
Tomorrow's Sunday!

Bianca Marsden (10)
Thames View Junior School

THE TITANIC

Water as cold as a freezer
Ship heavy as a planet
The ship going 55mph
It glides like a pond skater

People see an iceberg and rush to their captain
As the ship filled with water
And sank to the (?) bottom of the sea.

Aaron Prainer (11)
Thames View Junior School

THE JUNGLE

Wild creatures lurking,
Vultures scavenging for food,
Lions grooming young,
Eagles swooping down to their prey.

Snakes lie waiting for their prey,
Hippos widen their mouths.
Big, black, bears sniffing for food,
Monkeys swinging from vine to vine,
Searching in groups for the very best of nuts.

Elephants stand proudly,
Cheetahs lie comfortably under the shadow of the tree,
Young practise hunting, after their mum,
Birds sing majestically to soothe the jungle for the night.

Wale Odedoyin (11)
Thames View Junior School

THE INJECTION

'Will it hurt?'

'No, only as much as a pencil going through you.
You'll only scream as loud as the lady of screams.'

'There won't be much blood?'

'There won't be much blood.
Only as much as a chainsaw going through your head.
The needle is only as sharp as a shark's tooth.'

Dominic Wenman (9)
Thames View Junior School

THE WORLD IN A MARBLE

As I gaze through my marble, I see the
colour of green grass swaying in the wind
side by side.

As I peer through my marble, I see the colour
of a blue uniform, worn in our school.

As I gaze through my marble, I see the colour
of brown trees whistling in the wind.

As I peer through my marble I see the
colour of red bricks, built together.

As I gaze through my marble, I see the
colour of orange and yellow honey
sweet as sugar.

Jack Milburn (9)
Thames View Junior School

THE INJECTION

'Will it hurt?'

'No! Only as much as Jack the Ripper
stabbing you.
You will only scream as loud as if
you're being eaten by a shark.

There won't be much blood only
as much as the school being flooded!

The needle is only as long as a
sharp sword.'

Kurt Weatherley (10)
Thames View Junior School

THE STORM

The sky was a thick black velvet curtain,
Rain fell like darts aiming for the bullseye.
Clouds were like torrents of darkness, which
had spread their dark, midnight shade over us.
Naked trees swayed to and fro, some to the left
and some to the right.
Waves crashed against the rocks like roaring lions
trying to escape a cage.
The wind whistled and whirled and sliced
through the swaying naked trees.
Waves ferociously cut their way through
crumbling rocks.
A thick and low black cloud had covered
the sky and shadowed everywhere.

Leanne Scott (11)
Thames View Junior School

MARBLE

Marble, I see my fierce bear peer at me, I'm so scared.
The sky is blue, just like the sea.
My marble is dark, like a cloud or a castle.
I see my marble go
I know something's going to speak to me
I'm going to cry.
I saw my marble glow like gold.
I thought that I was rich
I saw birds fly around me with beautiful claws.

Jack Powell (9)
Thames View Junior School

MAGICAL COLOURS

Red is the colour of a bright red poppy field
growing really high or
red sweet blood that a vampire is
sucking out of someone's neck.

Blue is the colour of a dark blue whale
swimming in the aqua blue sea or
the colour of the dark blue jumpers
in Thames View.

White is the colour of an angel as it dances
across the starry night or
the colour of the white thick snow.

Fisayo Olabisi (10)
Thames View Junior School

THE JUNGLE

An arch of palm trees showing the way,
Calm, careful, cool,
Leaves, whirled, twirled and danced
In the air,
Falling, fragile, delicate.
Snakes strangling the tall dark trees.
Sparkling, shining, sleek.
A hole making a trap
Hollow, hell, hidden.
The jungle remained silent and still
For the next exploring visitor.
Waiting, whispering and watching.

Jodie Lee (11)
Thames View Junior School

THE WIND

The wind was a howling wolf
Throwing hats to the unkind floor
Sliced its way to the naked tree
Some were bent to the left, some to the right
The wind whistled and whirled
It threw everybody's house
The wind sniffed around the rooftops
It never stops . . .

Sabah Said (11)
Thames View Junior School

UNBELIEVABLE

There was an extensive rush of wind howling
while it was jumping from tree to tree.
A thick, velvety blanket was hanging over our heads.
There was a ribbon of moonlight.
Wolves were roaring while they were looking for immense prey.
Leaves were creeping across the dark, dusty, cobbled floors.

Daryl Skeels (11)
Thames View Junior School

RAINBOW

Brightly coloured among the clouds
Red, orange, yellow and green,
The sun was blazing through the trees
Pink, purple, blue were gracefully fading away,
But all that was left was a sudden glow of blue.

Kirsty Dyer (11)
Thames View Junior School

School Is Nonsense

My teacher's lovely.
Nonsense!
School can be fun
True!
School is nice because of teachers
Nonsense!
School would be better off without teachers.
True!
School would be better off with teachers.
Incorrect. Wrong! Nonsense, absolute rubbish!
False, untrue.
I tell you it's
Nonsense!
That's true!

Janie Stone (10)
Thames View Junior School

Storm At Sea

Crashing, crashing,
Colossal waves spray their water like a huge whale.
Scared, scared
As I sail the seven seas on my own.
Cold, cold
As the storm, as fierce as a lion, sliced its way through me.
Stranded, stranded
As I'm left to continue to travel the ocean's road.

Jenna Woods (11)
Thames View Junior School

THE COMET

Speeding, speeding through space,
A colossal chunk of rock
Travelling at great speed,
It might hit a planet
It might keep on travelling forever.

Andrew Puttnam (10)
Thames View Junior School

BEACH

Glistening gold sand shining in the sunlight
Azure blue sea, waves gently lapping,
Dark blue sky with frothy white clouds like ice cream
A golden coin tossed in the sky, shining over the beach.
Shells scattered along the golden sand.

Jemma Jeeves & Stephanie Swart (10)
Thames View Junior School

THE SEA

The soft gentle sea
Reflecting the milky white clouds.
As they float across summer azure skies.
The sea below is a dark tender blue.
The sun is like a blazing fireball
Sparkling like a diamond necklace.

Zoe Banton & Lauren Smith (11)
Thames View Junior School

The Lady Of England

One side, the stream quickly flows by
Crystal clear like the bright blue sky.
Peacefully through barley and rye,
Through barley and rye, roads run by,
The lady of England
Round the trees the children shall go,
Swimming in the pond as it flows,
As I fly low, I bang my toe
The island of Zanado.

Suzannah Dedman (11)
West Thurrock Primary School

Football Is . . .

Football is the best
No other sport is cool
Man Utd can beat the rest
Arsenal can't kick a ball
The best player in their team
Is of course, David Beckham
And another player that is keen
Is Teddy Sheringham.

Jamie Hanks (10)
West Thurrock Primary School

THE PLAYGROUND

In the playground
Near and far
Strange things happen
People lick their scars.

John is tall and skinny
Tim is big and fat
Andrew is a maniac
That has a French plait.

Lisa skips with her hair
Tommy plays football
Michael plays rounders
David bunks off school.

Mr Stan is stern but fair
He had vivid orange hair
Mr Colin is a geek
That doesn't really care.

At the whistle children line up
There becomes no sound
All is quiet
In the playground.

Regan Comer (11)
West Thurrock Primary School

MY BROTHER

My brother is such a pest
He's always saying he's the best.

He takes away my computer games,
Then throws them at the climbing frames.

My brother is extremely annoying
If I tell him to go away, he always starts crying.

He's always getting into trouble
By chewing gum then blowing a bubble.

Charlie Brain (10)
West Thurrock Primary School

THE THREE BILLY GOATS

In the meadow, goats eat grass,
Some goats race but there is one who is so fast.
While the river down below flows past,
One goat finds a neck cast.
Some are puffy,
Some are fluffy.

As they trot to find some grass,
Then they remember a bridge they had passed.
So they turn and run, as usual the youngest is last,
They get there and across the bridge there is grass.

Under the bridge, there is a troll,
Who has no soul.
He's mean and he's bad and eats a mole
He likes to play with dolls.

Carefully they cross
And then stopped at their cost.
The eldest knocks the troll off the bridge,
Then he dies from a cold and a cough.

Daniel Roberts (11)
West Thurrock Primary School

THE CAPTAIN OF GREAT YARMOUTH

On either side the soft sands lie
Where often the crabs tend to die
The sand makes children sleep and cry
While the lifeguard looks at the sky
The captain of Great Yarmouth.

All the families come and go
Most children tend to hurt their toe
Our fat tiny beach nurse is Mo
Her best friend is Giorgio
The guard of Great Yarmouth.

Zoe Lloyd (11)
West Thurrock Primary School

THE MASTER OF HOGWARTS

On either side the forest lie,
A river under a clear sky,
If you dare jump in, you shall die
And through the river, boats run by
To many-towered Hogwarts;
And back and forth the children go,
Hiding where the willows do grow
Feeling how slow the wind does blow
In the village of Hogsmeade.

David Taylor (11)
West Thurrock Primary School

Pigeons

They huddle in groups around the ground,
Making a funny squawking sound

They eat all scraps of bread and crisps,
Attracted to people with speaking lisps

Some pigeons are very tame,
And really could be full of fame

Pigeons are great creatures,
And have very beautiful features

People don't understand,
They can even eat from your hand

Pigeons.

Amy Ovel (10)
West Thurrock Primary School

The King Of Spain

On either side the countries lie
The heatwave gives a clear blue sky
When the people are walking by
The shiny hot sun makes them cry
The wonderful King of Spain.

People play in the swimming pool
While some people are keeping cool
Meanwhile their friends are at school
The famous King of Spain.

Danielle Williams (10)
West Thurrock Primary School

The Weather's Mood

The wind blows hard on the gusty trees
The waves crash on the rapid seas.

As the moon shines on the moor
That runs across the shiny floor.

As the moon turns around
The weather's mood calms down.

Now it's the end of the day
It is time for me to say
    Sleep well, sleep tight
    and hope that the
    weather's bright!

Reece Jarvis (11)
West Thurrock Primary School

My Family

My mum is an artist,
My dad goes from place to place,
My baby brother makes a mess
My older brother's still in school.

My dog won't stop barking,
My rat nibbles on the cage
My parrot won't stop talking
As for me, I'm just fine.

Karis Hill (10)
West Thurrock Primary School

THE KING OF ESSEX

On either side of the counties lie,
A long wide river which flows right by,
That reflects the sun and the sky
And you will see the people die,
When you see the town of Essex;
Round and round the people will go
To arrive in time for the show,
But no one knows the man below,
The king of mighty Essex.

Daisies whiten, roses quiver,
Little children stand and shiver,
By the train that runs forever
Over a bridge in the river
In the big town of Essex.
Near the trees that look like towers
Is a patch of tall white flowers,
And the silent town embowers
The tall king of Essex.

Andrew Gilbey (11)
West Thurrock Primary School

THE DAY I MET MY FRIENDS

As I walked up the street
I saw a big seat,
All my friends I went to meet.
We walked into the school and heard a beat
We saw some people having something to eat.
We saw a lot of running feet.
I saw my friends I was told to meet.

Della Rogers (11)
West Thurrock Primary School

Chips

Some people like them greasy,
All soaked in vinegar,
People think it's beastly
To eat with sliced pizza.

Chips, chips, lovely chips,
Leave the taste on your lips,
Leave a packet under Ted
Then at night, eat them in bed.

Some people think chips are great,
My dog doesn't care about a plate.
He eats them straight off the floor,
But I don't drop them anymore.

Chips, chips, lovely chips,
Leave the taste on your lips.
Leave a packet under Ted
Then at night, eat them in bed.

Thomas Morley (11)
West Thurrock Primary School

The Very First Step

Children walk on a winding stair
Side by side as a pair
We're going to a fair
We will see everyone there.
I can smell the fresh air
On the bed there was some hair.
In the zoo I saw a gigantic bear
My friend's sister is called Clair.

Leah Mead (10)
West Thurrock Primary School

Goldilocks

Three bears had brown hairs
And left eating three pears.

They had a bright house
And baby bear had a mouse.

They went into the gloomy woods
And smelled rotten hoods.

Baby bear was hungry
But his mum doesn't agree.

They went back to their house
And saw baby bear's mouse.

Kim Ormes (10)
West Thurrock Primary School

Trampolining

Bounce, bounce
turning around,
Bounce, bounce
high off the ground.
Bounce, bounce
I think I can fly,
Bounce, bounce
Up in the sky.
Seat drop, star jump
Straddle and tuck,
Time to get off.
What bad luck!

Rosie Brain (7)
West Thurrock Primary School

The Fly And The Green Frog

The fly flew across the sky,
He flew into a green frog's eye.

The green frog began to shout,
'That's my eye, get out, get out!'

The green frog said 'I want you for my tea'
The fly replied 'We will see.'

Just then the green frog sneezed, 'ah choo'
The fly escaped and said 'Thank you.'

Jerry Cosgrove (8)
West Thurrock Primary School

Witches' Bubbly Brew

Slurp and slop
Crackle and pop,
Lion's legs and mane
Eyeballs from a Great Dane.
Dragon's breath of fire
Ear from a liar.
From a cat: a nose,
From a cow: five toes,
A tooth of a bat
A bloodsucking gnat,
Slurp and slop
Crackle and pop.
The witches' bubbly brew
Is here for you!

Katie Graham (8)
William Read Primary School

London

This town makes me feel so small
Because the buildings are so tall,
There are parks and lakes and sights to see
With people selling things to me.

They sell things like mugs and paper flags
They even had the town of London on carrier bags,
They have shops and museums around the town
And in some places you might see some clowns.

There are the trains and buses too
Tower Bridge and London Zoo
There are lots of birds in Trafalgar Square
Well! There was when I was there!

Alfie Bernie Thomson (8)
William Read Primary School

Christmas Poem

Christmas is when you get presents,
Christmas is when you meet Santa.
Christmas is when you decorate your home
Christmas is going to a Christmas party
Christmas is happiness
Christmas is charity
Christmas is when you get a brand new Christmas tree
Christmas is remembering Jesus
Christmas is when you have Christmas dinner.

Raziye Sahan (8)
William Read Primary School

The Wizard's Spell

Triple, triple, boil and bubble;
Fire and flame, make some trouble.

Werewolf's hair and vampire's tooth
Ghost sweat and a boiled newt.

Crushed bugs and beetles' blood;
Bats' wings and a burning bud.

Frogs' eyes and human freckles
Leopard spots and blood that trickles.

Owl's wing and stuffed pig
Motor of a broken car and a giant's wig.

Monkey's brain and sheep's wool;
Toad skins and a very old ghoul.

Triple, triple, boil and bubble;
Fire, flames, make some trouble.

Callum Reed (9)
William Read Primary School

Magic Spells

Smoke and magic meet in the air
A sprinkling of pig's hair.
Eyeballs from a cute child
Add in animals from the wild.
Don't forget a goat's liver
And lots of snails that used to slither.
One last ingredient for my stew
What is it, do you wonder?
Well it's you!

Beth Craigie (9)
William Read Primary School

A Witch's Spell

A pinch of this
A pinch of that
Now to add the hairy one-eyed desert rat
Why should we add a brain or a bat
And there's the guts of a black cat
And let's add the grey wings of a gnat.

Patrick Mansfield (8)
William Read Primary School

The Witches' Spell

Double, hubble, make that bubble,
One puppy's eye and a bucket of trouble.
Rabbit ear boil,
Make a big ka-boom!
Lots of goo all over the room.

Zoe Blackwell (8)
William Read Primary School

Tiger! Tiger!

Growl! Growl!
Time for dinner
Eat a snake, eat a frog
I loved that jumping frog, delicious
Roar! Roar!

Samuel Faulks (8)
William Read Primary School

The Witches' Spell

Three ugly witches gather round a pot
They boil the water until it's hot
Now it's time to begin the spell
What they will add, no one can tell

In they throw a wing of a bat
And a furry leg of a cat
In next goes one whole dog
The potion bubbles up like fog

Cobwebs hang from the witches' hats
In they put six fat rats
An awful smell fills the room
The potion will be ready soon

When the sun begins to rise
Someone will be in for a nasty surprise
The witches have worked hard all night
Ready to deliver a great big fright!

Stephen Jones (8)
William Read Primary School

The Witches' Magic

Tiger's eyes and long rats' tails
Oh some slimy horrible snails
Some piglet's guts and slimed edible nuts
A dead rat and snorting cat
A snake that slithered
And a wand from a wizard
A baby's head and goat's legs
A bright frog
A snorting hog.

Connor Yarmouth (8)
William Read Primary School

THE WITCH'S POEM

Double, double, toil and trouble,
Put in a cauldron an eye from a dog,
Then add the skin of a big, brown frog.

Double, double, toil and trouble,
Add a pink ear from a dirty rat
And put in the tail of a smelly cat.

Double, double, toil and trouble,
Mix it up and make your wish,
Then serve it as a tasty dish.

Double, double, toil and trouble,
A spell is cast to make you run quick,
As long as you aren't sick, sick, sick.

Samantha Oldfield (8)
William Read Primary School

THE SPELL

Frog guts and puppy tongues added in with lizards' lungs
The liver of a pig, the skin of a snake.
The mouse got killed by the garden rake.
Heart from a shark
The water from a river.
The brain from a cow
Then the newt tried to slither.
Bulls' eyes and dogs' eyes
Mixed in as a dragon dies.
This is how the spell goes.
Ooops! I forgot some human toes.

Michael Boswell (9)
William Read Primary School

ALPHABET POEM

A is for ape who is strong
B is for bear who hits the gong
C is for camel who has got humps
D is for dragonfly who is always getting bumps
E is for elephant who makes a silly sound
F is for fox who lives in the pound
G is for gnat who bites your skin
H is for human who is thin as a pin
I is for igloo which is really stiff
J is for Joey who is always saying 'Biff!'
K is for kangaroo who jumps very high
L is for lady who is always saying 'Goodbye!'
M is for monkey who is using his key
N is for newt who is swimming at me
O is for octopus who is a star
P is for Peter who smokes a cigar
Q is for queen who is waiting to be crowned
R is for rainbow trout who is caught in a mound
S is for seal who is soft and grey
T is for tiger who is born in May
U is for unicorn who has a big horn
V is for vase that holds the corn
W is for whale who got stuck in the gnomes
X is for X-ray which shows your bones
Y is for yak who always moans
Z is for zebra who steps on the stones.

Amy Gregory (9)
William Read Primary School

The Witch's Spell

Double, double, toil and trouble,
Fire burn and cauldron bubble,
Leg of hare,
Mix and stir for a scare,
Tail of shrew,
Make it into an awful brew.
Frog's eye
And a pinch of a lie,
Wool of lamb,
Put it in with a slam.
Spines of a hedgehog
And a broken windowpane,
Double, double, toil and trouble,
Fire burn and cauldron bubble.

Johnathon Cuthbertson (8)
William Read Primary School

The Witches' Spell

Squashed flies and beetles' blood
brown leaves and soggy mud.
Frog's leg and bat wings
human eyes in it pings.
Owl's feet and gorillas' hair
slimy snails and a nightmare.
Sheep's brain and pigs' guts
Sticky glue and lions' cuts.
Sixteen teeth and a cat's saliva
wet pepper and a fish diver.

Amy Storey (9)
William Read Primary School

The Witch's Spell

Ar, la, dr, toil and bubble,
Fire ring, burn double,
Dead baby's rattle,
A live mouse's helmet from bottle,
Tadpole eyes,
Rabbit's green fur,
Pigs' mud from a sty,
Dark forest,
Hedgehog bones,
Tall trees,
Slimy stones,
An old magic spell
Should take it to hell,
Ar, la, dr, toil and bubble,
Fire ring, burn double.

Joshua Whenman (9)
William Read Primary School

The Witches' Spell

Witches' cauldron getting hot
Now to add into the pot
Frogs' legs and eyeballs
Bat wings and toes
Snot and bogies
That come from your nose.
Stir it altogether
And mix in a glass
Now serve it up
And give it to the class!

Danielle Kober (8)
William Read Primary School

THE WITCH'S SPELL

A magic spell to take someone to Hell
A smelly tail or a rat
A hairy wing of a bat.
A hedgehog's poisonous spine,
A bleeding leg of a porcupine.
Some stinking hair of a hare,
Some slimy skin off a pear
A magic spell
To take someone to Hell.

Carl Brampton (9)
William Read Primary School

WITCH'S SPELL

Hubble, hubble
Boys in trouble.
Monster's come to get you
And then he goes home.
The next day
He eats the two boys.

Carly Denham (8)
William Read Primary School

THE SPELL

Frog guts and frog legs and dead frogs and logs
and dogs' guts and a snakeskin with rats
and mice with some boots, hat, pens, dictionary,
paint, homework, sheet and a TV
with a little bit of a book in it.

Cheryl Bookless (9)
William Read Primary School

The Horrible Spell

Double, double, witches trouble
Frogs' guts and dogs' tongues
Lizard lungs and dirty thumbs
A slithery snake and a hairy tail
A pig's nose with wiggly toes
Rotten nails and crawling snails
Big fat flies and Mr Men ties
Crabs' legs and a thousand heads
Double, double, witches trouble.

Terri Hayward (8)
William Read Primary School

The Witches' Spell

In the forest there is trouble
And the cauldron is to bubble
In goes a toad or two
And one blob of frog's goo
A mouse's tail and some bones
And a bucket full of kittens' groans
A fox's tail is all we need
Now to make the frog bleed
Hula boom make this spell with a boom
And one stir with a tune
Now the spell is done with one big boom
In the forest there is trouble
And the cauldron is to bubble.

Victoria Jordan (9)
William Read Primary School

THE WITCH'S SPELL

Hubble bubble, nice and hot
Eleven fine things in my pot
A kitten's eye, three spiders' legs
A fruit bat's ears, twelve sparrow's eggs
A baby's liver
A rabbit's heart
A tiger's toe
A fat pig's fart
A lizard's tongue,
An elephant's shoe
And one last thing . . .
In goes you!

Toni Harris (9)
William Read Primary School

THE WITCH'S SPELL

Double, double, gruesome trouble,
Make the cauldron burn and bubble,
Now to add some crunchy bone,
Next to add the mobile phone.
Now I add a drippy nose,
And some smelly, cheesy toes.
Now to add a human brain,
And some horse's spiky mane.
Now to make it smell,
So it travels all the way to Hell.
Double, double, gruesome trouble,
Make the cauldron burn and bubble.

Natalie Pearson (9)
William Read Primary School

THE WITCH'S SPELL

Hubble, bubble, spoil and trouble,
Fire spit and cauldron bubble.
Slimy tongue from a school of dolphins,
Make them bake on a frying cauldron.
Body of bones,
Spiteful spikes of a hedgehog,
Beady eye of an eagle,
Sharp shavings from a log,
Huge lungs of a toad,
And a small leg of a shrew,
Iguana's green tail
And an animal that is new.

Matthew Doughty (9)
William Read Primary School

THE WITCH'S SPELL

Bubble, bubble, boiling rubble,
Nits and eyeball from fiddling twits,
Dead snake rattle, I love to battle,
In goes a hedgehog
And little bits of warthog.
Bubble, bubble, boiling rubble,
The beak of a swordfish,
Make a horrible wish,
The tongue from a porcupine
And voice box from a boy who was whining.
Bubble, bubble, boiling rubble.

Reid Manton (8)
William Read Primary School

THE WITCH'S SPELL

Witch stew, yucky cuboo
Eyeballs staring and floating around in the stew
Hedgehog spikes are spiking through
Blood from a snake is going into the brew
Brown and slimy snails are sinking to the bottom
Some soft and rough stones are going into the stew like cotton
A lung from a cat and a dog
A bit of steam and a bit of frog
A bit of this and a bit of that
And a bit of an old tattered hat
A dangerous bear and a bit of hair
So you'd better take care
Witch stew, yucky cuboo.

Amy Hayward (8)
William Read Primary School

THE WITCHES' SPELL

The witches tonight are making a bright spell.
They are going to take us to Hell.
They are going to use a lion's paw
And the end of a bird's claw.
They will boil it up and do a jig,
Jump up and down and add a pig.
Then they will add a tail of a hare,
And a tooth of a big bear.
They will stir and stir and make it hot,
Then give it to us to make us rot.

Jodi Placey (9)
William Read Primary School

THE WITCH'S SPELL

Double, double, gruesome trouble,
Fire burns, it will bubble.
Ear of puppy, bone from shark,
Little scales from a very big carp.
Add a little snail shell,
This is going to be hell.
Add a spine from a hedgehog.
A slimy eyeball from a frog,
Double, double, gruesome trouble,
Fire burns, it will bubble.

Victoria Waters (9)
William Read Primary School

THE WITCH'S SPELL

Trouble, trouble, burn and bubble,
It makes a lot of trouble.
Gooey eyeballs watching you,
Rabbits' hair with disgusting goo.
A big, long, coiled rattlesnake with slimy bones,
And rock-hard stones.
The witch's spell brings people to Hell,
And hear people shout with a *yell, yell!*
Trouble, trouble, burn and bubble,
It makes a lot of trouble.

Charlotte Fenwick (9)
William Read Primary School

The Witches' Spell

Make a terrible crushing sound,
Make it so it won't be found,
Add a little blood from this,
Add a snake and make it hiss,
Add some more crackling bones,
Add a lot of slimy stones,
Add a grisly bat's arm,
This spell isn't going to be calm,
Now we mix the gruesome spell
And fall into what we call hell.

Emily Dixon (8)
William Read Primary School

Going On A Journey

With our spacesuits on, we enter the rocket,
I give a kiss to my lucky locket.
We get into our seats and wait for blast-off,
To places that we've only ever dreamt of.
Walk on the moon, Jupiter and Mars,
Around the sun and the far away stars.
Talk to people from outer space,
People who look strange to the human race.
But I might be strange to them
And they might call me an alien.
I must be friendly, patient and kind,
And try to understand their minds.
No more time to think, we've got to go -
5, 4, 3, 2, 1, zero,
Blast-off! We're on our way,
I'll tell you about it when we come back one day.

Becky Moran (10)
Woodham Ley Primary School

WATER

Glistening in the light,
Calm as the night,
Until . . . splash,
We jump in,
It's very deep,
And cold,
Like jumping into a bowl of melted snow,
You dive in, it feels like silk,
When you're in the *water.*

Water bubbles,
Water is smooth,
You swim,
Play, and enjoy yourself,
You feel like a dolphin,
Swimming and gliding,
Up and down,
Round and round,
When you're in the *water.*

As clear as crystal,
As green as seaweed,
As cold as ice,
As warm as the summer sun,
You'll never know,
It's full of surprises,
It's waiting to joke,
So go on in,
It's *water.*

Kelly Crispin (10)
Woodham Ley Primary School

FASHION

Clothes and shoes,
Make-up and bags;
Just to look nice,
For seeing the lads.

Whether it's black,
Or whether it's white;
It can be worn,
Both day and night.

Your skirts are so short,
Your heels are so high,
Your make-up's so bright,
Just to catch a boy's eye.

Your bag is so small,
You can't fit it in;
That is the problem,
When your mobile rings!

Whatever you wear,
You're sure to look nice,
With sparkles and glitter,
They're sure to look twice!

Your nails are so long,
And painted so bright,
But remember the rule,
Try to be comfortable as well as so cool!

Siobhan Nicholls (11)
Woodham Ley Primary School

LOOKING OUT OF MY WINDOW

I look out of my window, staring at the stars,
Wondering where they come from
And wondering if they're far.

I look out of my window, staring at the moon,
Keeps changing shape,
Is it grey or blue?

I look out of my window, staring at the frost,
Wondering where it comes from
And why it is called frost.

I look out of my window, staring at the clouds,
Finding different shapes
And then I find a pound.

I am fed up with looking out of the window,
Where's my hat and coat?
I think I'll spend that pound I found,
Down the road I go.

Andrew Folkes (10)
Woodham Ley Primary School

THE MAN IN THE MOON

The man in the moon
Wakes up at noon
And goes to sleep at dawn.
In the night
The stars are bright,
And they sing
To the man in the moon.

Katie Larman (11)
Woodham Ley Primary School

The Haunted House

Ages and ages and ages ago,
I lived in a haunted house,
Where there were bats, rats, spiders and cats
And Scabbers, my pet mouse.

I was getting dressed in my bedroom,
Looking for something to wear,
When in came a hairy werewolf
And gave me quite a scare.

I decided to get some breakfast,
And join our friendly ghost,
So I cooked the bacon
And he did the toast.

Living there was lots of fun,
But Pa decided he'd had enough,
The mummy was too smelly
And the vampire was too rough.

Hannah Law (10)
Woodham Ley Primary School

Weekdays

On Monday it was a bluesday
Tuesday was the newsday
Wednesday was a confused day
Thursday was a used day
Friday was a who's who day
Saturday was a choose day
Sunday was rest day - that's my best day.

Kerry Siddle (10)
Woodham Ley Primary School

THE SCHOOL GHOST

The school ghost shrieked.
The children screamed.
The teachers made a run for it.
Ding-dong, ding-dong, the ghost rang the bell.
She slithered as she made her way down the corridor
And screamed in a high-pitched voice.
'Ha, ha, ha,' she cackled.
A ghost collector came and said,
'If I were you Ghost, I would run away now
Because I am going to catch you.'
'You wouldn't dare,' the ghost shrieked.
Bang! The ghost was caught.
The school was safe.
The children played while the teachers drank some whisky.

Kathryn Rossati (10)
Woodham Ley Primary School

SLEEPING IN MY BED

Sleeping in my comfy bed,
With a very loud buzzing in my head.
I'm floating in a paradise dream,
Of a chocolate and vanilla ice cream.

I wake up to see Mum and Dad,
But they are asleep and feeling bad.
I creep down the stairs as quiet as I dare,
There's no one around so I don't have to share.

Hannah Wright (10)
Woodham Ley Primary School

THE DARK NIGHT

The dark night is like a black hole,
Even as dark as a mole.
The moon is bright as a light,
It looks like it's going out of sight.
The red planet is called Mars,
It looks like a chocolate bar.
The night sky is completely plain,
It looks as if it's going to rain.
The shiny stars are so high,
The little stars look like diamonds in the sky.
The dark night looks like so many things,
The stars look like rings.
Dark night, dark night.

Fay Blowes (10)
Woodham Ley Primary School

TEACHER'S DRAWER

On Friday morning I sat with my toys,
All alone in the corner with the boys.
We walk to class,
Just about to pass,
The dreaded teacher's drawer.
Grabbing my toys with its claw,
I pull it back,
So it doesn't go into the black.

James Burton (10)
Woodham Ley Primary School

My Slimy Alien

His body is thin and bumpy, like rock,
His feet are spiky, no shape for a sock.
He has blue antennae and eight pink fairy wings,
He has eight round eyes, to see everything.
His brown body is the colour of mud,
His long, red tongue is the colour of blood.
His thin, scaly arms have an eye in each hand,
With four ears, two long, two short, he could hear a brass band!
He has black, short eyebrows and a spiky nose,
And his name is *Slimy* wherever he goes!

Leanne Goddard (9)
Woodham Ley Primary School

A Kitchen Drama

The fridge talks as it swings to and fro,
Dishes dance, forks clatter,
The fire on the stove burns freely as if it were alive,
Forks and dishes swim in the sink before being washed,
Water trickles and squeaks as it goes down the drain,
The cooker looks around with happy, gleaming eyes,
Teacups hide behind the dishes as if to play hide and seek,
The drawers rush out like they're missing something,
And then it goes silent once again.

Dan Cuthbert (10)
Woodham Ley Primary School

Spring

Orange sunshine glows
    wind blows
The clouds are white
Fresh grass comes up
    flowers grow
Daffodils open
Tulips say hello
    birds sing
Butterflies flutter
Lambs awake
Trees whistle
Children play.

Sammie Looker (10)
Woodham Ley Primary School

I Wanna Be Very Cool

I wanna be very cool,
I wanna dive into a massive pool,
A back flip would be very good,
But I don't know if I should,
If I fail I shall look a fool,
If I succeed I shall look very cool,
I wanna be very cool!

Jordan Cutting (10)
Woodham Ley Primary School

The Colour Blue

The colour blue is marvellous,
The colour blue is devious,
The colour blue is the colour of sea,
The colour blue is my personality,
The colour blue is a fantasy,
The colour blue is a maze to me,
The colour blue is the colour of the sky,
The colour blue is a bird flying high,
The colour blue is the colour of my eyes,
The colour blue is the colour of ties.

Hayley Wood (10)
Woodham Ley Primary School

Days Of The Week

On Monday I flew into outer space,
On Tuesday I joined the human race,
On Wednesday I had a dirty face,
On Thursday I had a game of chase,
On Friday I went to my friend's place,
On Saturday I played cards and won with an ace,
On Sunday at dinner I wouldn't say grace,
And that's the end of my weekend disgrace.

Penny Barrett (10)
Woodham Ley Primary School

A Busy Class

A t school I've got a really
B ossy teacher, who
C an always give you a
D etention for doing the smallest thing,
E ven dropping a drawing pencil,
F or
G oodness sake,
H ow strict can you get?
I really hate her, so does my mate,
J o. Most of the boys aim a pretend
K ick behind her back, which makes us
L augh, which
M ight even get us a-
N other detention,
O r she might even ring up our
P arents, which would be really terrible. She always likes to shout,
'Q uiet in the class-
R oom,' or even
'S ilence!'
T hen, when she turns her back on
U s, we can see a
V ein throbbing in the side of her head.
W hen the bell goes, I run home ready for my
X ylophone lesson and hope that I won't be late tomorrow like I was
Y esterday for the
Z oo trip. I wish I had missed the whole day!

Lynsey Newman (10)
Woodham Ley Primary School